CORPORATE RESPONSIBILITY
AND
FINANCIAL PERFORMANCE

CORPORATE RESPONSIBILITY AND FINANCIAL PERFORMANCE

The Paradox of Social Cost

Moses L. Pava
Joshua Krausz

QUORUM BOOKS
Westport, Connecticut • London

Library of Congress Cataloging-in-Publication Data

Pava, Moses L.
   Corporate responsibility and financial performance : the paradox
of social cost / Moses L. Pava, Joshua Krausz.
      p.   cm.
   Includes bibliographical references and index.
   ISBN 0–89930–921–6
   1. Social responsibility of business. 2. Social responsibility of
business—Costs. 3. Corporations—Finance. I. Krausz, Joshua.
II. Title.
HD60.P33   1995
658.4'08—dc20   94–45284

British Library Cataloguing in Publication Data is available.

Library of Congress Catalog Card Number: 94–45284
ISBN: 0–89930–921–6

First published in 1995

Quorum Books, 88 Post Road West, Westport, CT 06881
An imprint of Greenwood Publishing Group, Inc.

Printed in the United States of America

The paper used in this book complies with the
Permanent Paper Standard issued by the National
Information Standards Organization (Z39.48–1984).

10 9 8 7 6 5 4 3 2 1

Copyright Acknowledgments

The authors and the publisher gratefully acknowledge permission to reprint excerpts
from previously published material.

Selected excerpts from *The New Realities* by Peter F. Drucker. Copyright © 1989 by
Peter F. Drucker. Reprinted by permission of HarperCollins Publishers Inc.

Excerpts from "Information Disclosure Strategy" by Baruch Lev. Copyright © 1992 by
The Regents of the University of California. Reprinted from the *California
Management Review*, Vol. 34, No. 4. By permission of The Regents.

Selected excerpts from *Where the Law Ends: The Social Control of Corporate
Behaviour* by Christopher Stone. Copyright © 1975 by Christopher Stone. Reprinted
by permission of HarperCollins Publishers, Inc.

To V.B.N. and M.K.

Contents

I
The Association between Corporate Social
Responsibility and Financial Performance

II
The Language of Corporate Social Responsibility

Contents

III
The Legitimacy of Corporate Social Responsibility

Tables

Acknowledgments

This research project was funded, in part, by a generous grant from The Lupin Foundation. We would especially like to thank the founding dean of the Sy Syms School of Business, Michael Schiff, for his guidance and wisdom in helping develop the research agenda, and our current dean, Harold Nierenberg, for providing an environment conducive to completing this project.

We have gained much from the opportunities we have had to share our findings with colleagues and friends. We thank the participants at the 1994 International Association for Business and Society Annual Conference, the 1994 meeting of the Academy of Business Administration, and the 1994 Northeast and Mid-Atlantic American Accounting Association meetings. The responses that we have received from our colleagues have been both elucidating and encouraging.

Colleagues, administrators, and staff at Yeshiva University have been especially helpful. We thank President Norman Lamm and Vice President of Academic Affairs William Schwartz. Aaron Levine has been extremely helpful in helping us clarify our thoughts on corporate social responsibility. We will be forever grateful to Clarence Walton, who served as the Distinguished Visiting Professor and Kukin Chairholder at the Syms School during the 1993 winter term. In both word and deed, Walton has been a model to emulate. His teaching and scholarship have profoundly influenced this book.

We also thank Joshua Livnat, Ron Goetzel, Ellen Dorosh, and Marcy Weiner for their constant encouragement, practical advice, and sensitive help.

Ultimately, this book would not have been written without the continuous wisdom, common sense, and love of our wives. Together with our wives and families we daily explore the real meaning and impact of social responsibility. It is to our wives that this book is dedicated.

1

Introduction:
The Idea of Corporate
Social Responsibility

The idea of corporate social responsibility (CSR) is neither new nor radical. The core belief is that the corporation incurs responsibilities to society beyond profit maximization. Huge corporations possess the power to control and influence the quality of life of employees, customers, shareholders, and residents of local communities in which they operate. A single corporate decision can irrevocably change the lives of thousands of people. Power necessarily entails responsibility. Managers, in pursuing their primary goal of increasing shareholder value, have social responsibilities beyond meeting the minimal requirements of the law. As early as 1916, J. Maurice Clark, writing in the *Journal of Political Economy*, noted that "if men are responsible for the known results of their actions, business responsibilities must include the known results of business dealings, whether these have been recognized by law or not" (p. 223).

SOME CASES IN CORPORATE
SOCIAL RESPONSIBILITY

Some recent cases illustrate the importance of CSR:

Case 1: The New York *Times* recently reported that a gun producer will begin manufacturing a new bullet that, after entering the body, explodes inside the victim, making it almost impossible for a doctor to surgically remove.

Case 2: Last year a record company faced intense public pressure over its release of an album advocating the killing of police officers.

Case 3: A few years ago a beer distillery was severely criticized for specifically marketing a high-alcohol malt liquor in poor urban areas.

Case 4: An important national newspaper refused a request to refrain from publishing advertisements from the Kingdom of Saudi Arabia (which is openly anti-semitic and sexist in its employment practices), arguing that it would not pursue its editorial policy through the acceptance or non-acceptance of advertising.

Case 5: During the 1960s, the research department of a tobacco company developed a safer, less toxic cigarette. Company officials never marketed the cigarette, and decided later to eliminate the research department. High-level executives in the industry publicly claim that no scientific evidence exists to prove a cause and effect relationship between cigarette smoking and health hazards.

Can and should managers in these corporations explore the ethical and moral responsibilities of their business decisions? Does there exist a class of cases where managers should forego profits in order to pursue perceived social responsibilities?

Advocates for increased CSR believe that the answers to these questions are obvious. Even if management is convinced that long run profits might be enhanced by the production of a technologically sophisticated bullet, managers and directors have a right and an obligation to say no. Managers of record companies and beer distilleries must consider both the financial and ethical implications of marketing their products. It is justifiable for a newspaper, especially a newspaper that advocates increased CSR for other businesses, to pursue business practices consistent with its editorial policy. A tobacco company has an ethical obligation to pursue research aimed at minimizing the health problems caused by cigarette smoking. In each of these five cases, business managers must consider the unique ethical and moral responsibilities of the corporation.

In his book *The Moral Manager* (1988), Clarence C. Walton describes the organizational philosophy underlying the pro-social responsibility movement as "covenant ethics," as opposed to "contract ethics." Walton notes, "The covenant model . . . draws much of its inspiration from religion and places people above pockets: to belong to a community is to have claims upon it" (p. 209). He goes on to argue that the advantage of the covenant model "is that it invites leaders to take a large view of their responsibilities because, under it, corporations are seen as much as moral organizations as they are money-making machines" (p. 210). Importantly, Walton is careful not to overstate the case for CSR. For example, even while he advocates the covenant approach, he clearly describes the benefits of a classical contractual approach:

To define the covenant model as humanitarian and the contract model as narrowly economic is misplaced. Contractualists are also interested in humans. What they say is that the fruits of organzied efforts should be allocated strictly on the basis of contributions and since one normally cannot hire workers without first securing capital, providers of capital come first. Furthermore, in today's world and particularly in large organizations, principals often come out a poor second. Agents can and do negotiate deals with substantial, if not total, indifference toward the principals: doctors use hospitals for their own practices; professors exploit institutional prestige to secure lucrative consulting assignments; and managers run fantastic aerial displays with golden parachutes. When concern for principals is minimized, injustices occur. (p. 209)

Underlying the pro-social responsibility view is the belief that legal solutions are not always sufficient. Advocates for increased social responsibility point out the limitations inherent in a complete reliance on the law. Christopher D. Stone, in his book *Where the Law Ends: The Social Control of Corporate Behavior* (1975), provides the most exhaustive discussion of this topic. Stone describes general reasons why the law is limited in terms of what it can accomplish. Among his reasons are the time lag problem and limitations connected with making and implementing the law.

The time lag problem suggests that the law is "primarily a reactive institution" (p. 94). Therefore, there may exist a significant period of time between when a problem is recognized and when the legislature can pass a law to solve the problem. Until new laws are passed "a great deal of damage — some irreversible — can be done" (p. 94). Socially responsible managers, therefore, should not exploit a situation and quickly engage in an activity when the legislature simply has not had time to act.

One of the most important problems associated with limitations connected with making the law is the significant information gap that exists between legislators and corporate managers. Stone makes the point as follows:

But when we attempt to legislate in more complex areas, we find an information gap. Even the specialized regulatory agencies, much less the Congress, cannot in their rule-making capacities keep technically abreast of the industry. Are employees who work around asbestos being subjected to high risks of cancer? What psychological and physical dangers lurk in various forms of manufacturing processes? . . . Congress and the various regulatory bodies can barely begin to answer these questions. The companies most closely associated with the problems may not know the answers either; but they certainly have the more ready access to the most probative information. (p. 96)

Again, it is unthinkable that corporate managers should engage in activities that the legislature, if it possessed the same information as management, would undoubtedly prohibit.

Stone, in line with other pro-social responsibility advocates, concludes his survey by writing as follows: "If the agencies — or the other public control mechanisms — were effective, then it would be proper to brush aside the calls for corporate social responsibility by calling on the law to keep corporations in line. But the weaknesses of the agencies are simply a further argument that trust in our traditional legal machinery as a means of keeping corporations in bounds is misplaced — and that therefore something more is needed" (p. 110). That something more is, of course, increased social responsibility on the part of corporations.

A BRIEF HISTORY

Corporate social responsibility, as discussed in this book, is primarily a twentieth-century invention, though its ancient and venerable roots can be traced easily to Biblical sources. The concept is evident, for example, in Deuteronomy 24:10–13 and 25:13–16. The twentieth century has seen an unprecedented growth in the size, importance, and power of the corporation. Corporations have proven to be extremely efficient at producing goods and services. It is the success of the corporation that has necessitated the development of the idea of CSR.

Adolf A. Berle, Jr. and Gardiner C. Means, both at Columbia University, were among the earliest business researchers to explain and formally document the revolutionary changes that had taken place in the U.S. economy. In their pathfinding work, *The Modern Corporation and Private Property*, published in 1933, the authors warned readers about the increasing power of corporate managers:

Such a great concentration of power and such a diversity of interest raise the long-fought issue of power and its regulation — of interest and its protection. A constant warfare has existed between the individuals wielding power, in whatever form, and the subjects of that power. Just as there is a continuous desire for power, so also there is a continuous desire to make that power the servant of the bulk of the individuals it affects. . . . Absolute power is useful in building the organization. More slow, but equally sure is the development of social pressure demanding that the power shall be used for the benefit of all concerned. This pressure, constant in ecclesiastical and political history, is already making its appearance in many guises in the economic field. (p. 353)

Further, Berle and Means carefully noted the failure of traditional views of the corporation:

By tradition, a corporation "belongs" to its shareholders . . . and theirs is the only interest to be recognized as the object of corporate activity. Following this tradition, and without regard for the changed character of ownership, it would be possible to apply in the interests of the passive property owner the doctrine of strict property rights. . . . By application of this doctrine, the group in control of a corporation would be placed in a position of trusteeship in which it would be called on to operate or arrange for the operation of the corporation for the sole benefit of the security owners despite the fact that the latter have ceased to have power over or to accept responsibility for the active property in which they have an interest. Were this course followed, the bulk of American industry might soon be operated by trustees for the sole benefit of inactive and irresponsible security owners. (p. 354)

Berle and Means concluded their study with prophetic accuracy. They wrote, "Neither the claims of ownership nor those of control can stand against the paramount interests of the community" (p. 356).

In a later work, Berle (1954) clarified this more boldly. In order to meet the demands of society, corporations need to demonstrate self-restraint. Although Berle chose to use the term "corporate conscience," his view unquestionably represents an important early articulation of CSR:

So, it seems, the corporations have a conscience, or else accept direction from the conscience of the government. This conscience must be built into institutions so that it can be invoked as a right by the individuals and interests subject to the corporate power. It may not be christened with a Latin name; its keeper may not be called "Chancellor," the place where the conscience can be called into action will no longer be called the Curia Regis. But, as at Runnymede through Magna Carta, it will be required to be present and reachable. It will be required to observe certain rules designed for the protection of individuals. (p. 114)

Berle's view is correct. In fact, much of the history of corporate social responsiblity has been an attempt to experiment with alternative ways of institutionalizing the corporate conscience. Individuals and groups, both inside and outside the corporation, have recognized the special status of corporations and their unique social responsibilities. These business leaders and critics have tried to formulate a coherent view of the corporation that attempts to take both the profit motive and legitimate social goals seriously.

Morrell Heald (1957) reviewed numerous statements and policies of corporate executives from the early part of this century. Among some of the examples cited are the following: the Colorado Fuel and Iron Company publicly announced that the very purpose of the enterprise was "to solve the social problem" (p. 377). Anticipating the academic work of Berle and Means discussed above, George W. Perkins, a director of U.S. Steel and International Harvester, stated in 1908, "The larger the corporation becomes, the greater become its responsiblities to the entire community" (p. 378). In the 1913 Annual Report, the chief executive officer of the Bell System, Theodore N. Vail, wrote that, "We feel our obligation to the general public as strongly as to our investing public, or to our own personal interests" (p. 378). John D. Rockefeller, Jr., writing in 1923, sensed the changing environment: "Shall we cling to the conception of industry as an instituion primarily of private interests, which enables certain individuals to accumulate wealth, too often irrespective of the well-being, the health, and the happiness of those engaged in its production? Or shall we adopt the modern viewpoint and regard industry as being a form of social service, quite as much as a revenue-producing process?" (p. 378). Rockefeller continued that the old order was past. "To cling to such a conception is only to arouse antagonisms and to court trouble. In the light of the present every thoughtful man must concede that the purpose of industry is quite as much the advancement of social well-being as the production of wealth" (p. 380).

Unquestionably these pronouncements represent a minority view. Readers, then as now, are entitled to a healthy skepticism. It is, of course, impossible to gauge the credibility of these statements. Nevertheless, the fact that business leaders felt a need to avoid "antagonisms," as Rockefeller put it, underscores the very real political changes that were taking place. Whether or not his "thoughtful man" concedes that the purpose of industry "is the advancement of social well-being" for purely utilitarian purposes is not crucial. The idea of a social responsiblity is, in a sense, independent of the motives of those individuals who articulated it. A cynic might put it as follows: corporate activities, for all practical purposes, need to satisfy social responsibilities as if they might really exist.

In addition to these early initiatives of corporate leaders, more recent instances of shareholders exerting pressure on the corporation have been documented. At its 1967 annual meeting, for example, Eastman Kodak Company executives faced a difficult predicament after a company vice-president first made, then reneged on a promise to provide additional jobs for minority residents of Rochester, New York. A coalition of black activists mobilized hundreds of shareholders in an attempt to get the company to honor its earlier commitment. The activists and the company eventually reached a compromise. Other companies have also faced shareholder opposition on social responsibility issues. Chase Manhattan and First National City banks faced pressure from institu-tional shareholders for their South African connections. Dow Chemical Company faced intense scrutiny for producing napalm. Honeywell was criticized for its production of antipersonnel weapons used in the Vietnam War. In response to public pressure, Whirlpool stopped accepting military contracts. During the 1970s, numerous groups began placing public interest resolutions on the proxy statements of targeted corporations. For example, the corporate governance at General Motors was directly challenged. Even more recently, pension funds have begun to take more active roles in the area of CSR. For example, the California pension fund recently announced that it would screen companies based on management and employee relationships.

MOTIVATION FOR THIS STUDY

This brief historical sketch is not meant to be exhaustive, but rather illustrative. The examples catalogued above could be multiplied easily. The core idea of CSR, the notion that companies have a responsibility beyond legal requirements, is by now deeply embedded in the corporate cultures of the largest U.S. companies. Our major conclusion, based on the historical record, can be summarized as follows: at this stage, we believe that the question of whether or not corporations have a social responsibility has already been answered affirmatively. It is much more interesting and productive to focus on the following two issues. First, how do existing CSR programs affect the corporation? Second, what constitutes the precise contours of this responsibility? The purpose of this book is to explore these two themes.

The issue of how CSR affects individual companies engaged in these activities is not well understood. Further, the distinction between legitimate and illegitimate CSR activities has not always been clearly drawn. This book, therefore, is designed to fill in some of the gaps in our understanding. We do this by carefully organizing and reviewing the relevant and growing literature on CSR. In addition, this book reports on the results of two original empirical studies designed to further explore the notion of CSR.

OVERVIEW

The book is divided into three parts. Part I examines the relationship between social responsibility and financial performance. Chapter 2 provides an extensive literature review of this topic. The main conclusion of this chapter is our observation that, of the 21 previously published empirical studies identified, 12 reported a positive association between social resopnsibility and financial performance, 1 reported a negative association, and 8 reported no measurable association. While it is evidently true that not all studies report that socially responsible firms perform better than non-socially responsible firms, the overwhelming evidence indicates that these firms perform at least as well as other firms. We believe that this finding directly contradicts the traditionalist view of the corporation. This surprising empirical regularity constitutes *prima facie* evidence for the existence of what we term the "paradox of social cost." To the extent that social activities are costly to the firm (even while creating positive externalities), one would predict a negative relationshp between social performance and financial performance at the individual firm level. In Chapter 3, we provide original evidence suggesting that the positive association may be explained by a causal link between social responsibility and financial performance. Specifically, we examine the long-term financial prformance of a group of 53 firms that have been identified by the Council on Economic Priorities as meeting socially responsible criteria and compare their performance to a control sample matched by both industry and size. In addition, to test for changes over time, we compare the relative performance of these two groups of firms in two time periods (1985–87 and 1989–91). With appropriate qualifications, we conclude that social responsibility sometimes causes better financial performance.

In addition to examining the link between social responsibility and financial performance, in Part II we extend our empirical analysis and look at the relationship between social responsibility and information disclosure. The purpose of this second phase of the study is to investigate and measure annual report disclosures of social responsibility activities for the sample of firms that had previously been identified as meeting CSR criteria. We compare these results to an analysis of social responsibility disclosures for the control sample. Chapter 4 surveys prior research on this topic, and Chapter 5 specifies the methodology and results. We conclude Part II by noting that a positive association between actual performance and disclosures characterizes the relationship.

In parts I and II of this book the issue of legitimacy is taken for granted. While this working assumption is useful for generating our empirical results, in Part III the issue of legitimacy is explored more fully. The specific goal of Chapter 6 is to provide the reader with a general discussion about the legitimacy of CSR. Specifically, the chapter discusses four distinct criteria for evaluating the legitimacy of corporate projects for institutionalizing social responsibility: local knowledge, level of responsibility, shared consensus, and relationship to financial performance. In Chapter 7 these criteria are applied to five specific social responsibility projects. The analysis in this chapter sheds further light on the criteria developed in the previous chapter and allows us to draw specific conclusions about some (but certainly not all) of the important institutional projects relevant to CSR. Chapter 8 continues this discussion by examining corporate responsibilities in the area of information disclosure. This discussion is important because it reminds us that, while there is often a link between social responsibility and financial performance as discussed in chapters 6 and 7, this link is neither necessary nor sufficient for evaluating the legitimacy of CSR. Finally, Chapter 9 summarizes our findings. We articulate our major observations in the form of ten propositions. In selecting the ten propositions discussed in Chapter 9, our goal is to provide a summary of the most important implications of over 20 years of empirical and theoretical research. Although the discussion moves from less to more controversial aspects of CSR, we highlight those areas in which there is a high degree of consensus.

We conclude this introduction by quoting from the philosopher Alisdair MacIntyre, in his book *After Virtue*:

Man in his actions and practice, as well as in his fictions, is essentially a story-telling animal. He is not essentially, but becomes through his history, a teller of stories that aspire to truth. But the key question for men is not about their own authorship; I can only answer the question "What am I to do?" if I can answer the prior question "Of what story or stories do I find myself a part?" We enter human society, that is, with one or more imputed characters — roles into which we have been drafted — and we have to learn what they are in order to be able to understand how others respond to us and how our responses to them are apt to be construed. (p. 201)

MacIntyre's observation about individual human behavior applies at the organizational level as well. A corporation can only answer the question "What are we to do?" if it can answer the prior question "Of what story or stories do we find ourselves a part?" This book, although rigorous and technical in style, in a very real sense is about the appropriate roles and stories that we ourselves are currently creating for the corporation. As we evolve beyond the view of simple profit maximization, the call for increased CSR becomes more urgent.

I

THE ASSOCIATION BETWEEN CORPORATE SOCIAL RESPONSIBILITY AND FINANCIAL PERFORMANCE

Organizations have to take "social responsibility." There is no one else around in the society of organizations to take care of society itself. Yet they must do so responsibly, within the limits of their competence, and without endangering their performance capacity.

— Drucker, 1993, p. 97

2

The Paradox of Social Cost

It is generally assumed that common stock investors are exclusively interested in earning the highest level of future cash flow for a given amount of risk. This view suggests that investors select a well-diversified portfolio of securities to achieve this goal. Accordingly, it is often assumed that investors are unwilling to pay a premium for corporate behavior that can be described as socially responsible. Under the traditional view, to the extent that corporations engage in costly behavior to achieve socially responsible goals that cannot be translated into higher cash flow in the future, investors would be expected to place a lower value on corporate securities.

Recently, this view has been under increasing attack. Apparently, many investors, including both large institutional investors and individual investors, are concerned about a much larger set of corporate priorities. According to the Social Investment Forum, at least 538 institutional investors now allocate funds using social screens or criteria. For example, the Teachers Insurance and Annuity Association and College Retirement and Equities Fund, with assets of about $9 billion, uses corporate social responsibility (CSR) performance as an additional screen in making investment decisions. In addition, there are now numerous mutual funds that are designed to satisfy the demands of socially responsible investors. A study by the United States Trust Company of Boston conservatively estimated that at the end of 1985 about $100 billion in funds were managed under at least one form of social criteria. Mitchell Investment Management, using a less conservative procedure, estimated that there were $220 billion in funds managed under South African criteria alone (Baldwin, et al., 1986). Alice Tepper Marlin, president of the New York-based Council on Economic Priorities (CEP), has more recently estimated that more than $600 billion of invested funds are socially screened (1992).

While the notion of socially responsible investing is often a vague and ill-defined concept and, therefore, extremely difficult to quantify, there is, nevertheless, a cluster of core issues that describes the practice. Among the most common issues are environmental concerns, community relations, military contracts, nuclear energy, product quality, consumer relations, employee relations, philanthropy, and South African investments.

There are many other issues that individual investors might use in classifying corporations as socially responsible. One important example is the issue of the economic boycott of Israel. Many individual investors might eliminate a company from their portfolio if they were aware that the company had either a formal or informal policy of not doing business with Israel. Because of the absence of this issue and many others, it is important to recognize that, while socially responsible investing represents an economic philosophy, in practice it also tends to correlate with a political world view. Screening on the basis of social responsibility refers merely to those rules that current practitioners employ in selecting corporate investments, in addition to the traditional economic screens. In this sense, it is a descriptive term only. It also should be noted that scoring high along one of the nine core issues is not always perceived as evidence of socially responsible behavior. For example, companies in the drug industry have historically donated large amounts of money to hospitals as philanthropic contributions. Drug firms, which have traditionally been perceived as socially responsible, may now find themselves under more intense scrutiny and may have to explain more precisely the rationale for such giving, which one drug company labels as strategic. According to a recent New York *Times* article, for example, in a political climate in which an increasing percentage of gross domestic product is being allocated to health care costs, drug firms should consider curtailing charitable contributions in order to lower product costs (February 22, 1993). In the drug industry, concern for the consumer, and more general concern for the robustness of the economy as a whole, may trump charitable giving as socially responsible activities.

Although the practice of using both traditional economic criteria and social responsibility screens to allocate funds is becoming more common, and while the legal constraints associated with the practice are apparently being removed, the implications are still not well understood.[1] What are its financial benefits and costs? Is there a measurable financial impact?

The objectives of this study are threefold. First, in the next section, we will review over 20 empirical studies that have attempted to measure both the direction and the degree of association between CSR and financial performance. Second, because of limitations inherent in the previous work, we further explore the association between CSR and traditional financial performance. In this study, we examine the long-term financial performance of a group of 53 firms that have been identified by the CEP as being socially responsible and compare the financial performance of this group to a control sample matched by size and industry (Council on Economic Priorities et al., 1991). The rationale for basing our study on the CEP firms will be discussed in Chapter 3, where we describe the methodology and results of the study. Third, and most importantly, we hope that by further studying the statistical association between CSR and financial performance, we will shed additional light on both the benefits and the costs associated with socially responsible actions. In this way we intend to formulate a better understanding of the nature and limitations of CSR. We believe that our conclusions have important implications for academics, investors, and corporate executives.

THE ASSOCIATION BETWEEN CORPORATE SOCIAL RESPONSIBILITY AND FINANCIAL PERFORMANCE: THE EVIDENCE

In an attempt to understand the relationship between CSR and financial performance, there have been numerous studies that have measured the statistical association between perceived CSR and traditional financial performance. We have identified and reviewed 21 empirical studies that explicitly addressed this question as the major research objective. Our investigation reveals an important, and, we believe, unappreciated, empirical regularity. Succinctly stated, nearly all empirical studies to date have concluded that firms that are perceived as having met social responsibility criteria have either outperformed or performed as well as other firms that are not necessarily socially responsible.

This surprising empirical regularity, which we label the "paradox of social cost," demands an explanation. To the extent that social activities are costly to the firm (even while creating positive externalities), one would expect a negative relationship between social performance and financial performance at the individual firm level.

THE TRADITIONALIST VIEW
OF THE CORPORATION

Milton Friedman is most closely associated with the traditional view of the corporation (see M. Friedman, 1962 and 1970; M. Friedman and R. Friedman, 1980). His position can be summarized as follows: business managers have a responsibility to shareholders — the owners of the corporation — to maximize firm value. Managers, acting as agents of the shareholders, have no mandate to embark on socially responsible projects that do not enhance the income-generating ability of the firm. In addition, managers should not refrain from profitable investments that satisfy all legal constraints but do not conform to the manager's own personal social agenda. Rather, as Friedman put it, "The social responsibility of business is to increase profits." He further emphasized, "Few trends would so thoroughly undermine the very foundations of our free society as the acceptance by corporate officials of a social responsibility other than to make as much money for their stockholders as they possibly can. This is a fundamentally subversive doctrine" (1962, p. 133).

Friedman's primary assumption that leads to his conclusion that CSR is a "subversive doctrine" is his belief that the term "social responsibility," as applied to the corporate context, if it means anything at all, implies that the business manager "must act in some way that is not in the interest of his employers" (1970, p. 33). Thus, managers who act out of a sense of social responsibility are engaging in a form of taxation without representation.

Further, Friedman believes that business managers have no comparative advantage when it comes to implementing social programs. Managers are experts in producing products, selling them, or financing them. Management has no necessary expertise in fighting social ills.

We believe that Friedman's argument is both rigorous and somewhat convincing. His voice, although the loudest, clearest, and least apologetic, is by no means solitary.[2] Numerous economists, accountants, sociologists, corporate executives, and social critics either explicitly or implicitly accept a similar view of the corporation.

Hawley (1991), for example, surveyed 22 corporate finance textbooks in order to determine the authors' perceptions of the "goal of the corporate manager." The author concluded:

The typical Introductory Corporate Finance course begins with the instructor posing the following question to the students: "What is the primary objective of financial managers and the corporation?" The answer, of course, is that corporate managers should seek to maximize the wealth of owners by maximizing the price of the common shares. This concept of shareholder wealth maximization (SWM) then pervades the rest of the course. It is presented as the basis for the most important decisions that financial managers must make for the corporation, including the selection of capital investments, setting the capital structure, and acquiring or divesting strategic units. Furthermore, it is defended as the primary objective of the corporation and all of its managers, not just financial managers. (p. 712)

Hawley's conclusions are not unexpected. After all, the Capital Asset Pricing Model (CAPM), a foundation of modern finance, assumes that investors are concerned with only two relevant characteristics — the mean and variance of portfolio returns. Foster (1986) described the assumptions of CAPM as follows: "Two key assumptions about investor preferences underlie CAPM: 1. Two statistics, the mean and variance, are sufficient to describe investor preferences over the distribution of future returns on a portfolio. 2. Investors prefer higher expected returns to lower expected returns for a given level of portfolio variance, and prefer lower variance to higher variance of portfolio returns for a given level of expected returns" (p. 337).

Empirical studies often assume the traditionalist view as a starting point. For example, Baldwin and colleagues (1986), in investigating the relationship between CSR and financial performance, wrote that the purpose of their study was to produce quantitative estimates of the penalty, as non-market risk, that investors would have to bear as a result of not being able to invest in various equity securities. The implicit assumption is that there must be a cost. The only relevant question remaining, according to these authors, is whether the cost is material.

Accounting regulators have accepted the traditional view of the corporation as described by economists. They have gone so far as to codify this view by including the following discussion in the Concepts Project that was designed as the accounting regulators "constitution":

Potential users of financial information most directly concerned with a particular business enterprise are generally interested in its ability to generate favorable cash flows because their decisions relate to amounts, timing, and uncertainties of expected cash flows. To investors, lenders, suppliers, and employees, a business enterprise is a source of cash in the form of dividends or interest and perhaps appreciated market prices, repayment of borrowing, payment for goods or services, or salaries or wages. (Financial Accounting Standards Board Concept No. 1, par. 25, issued November 1978)

The observations included in this paragraph that described the functions of a corporation provide a revealing glimpse into how accountants generally perceive the role of the corporation.

Economists and accountants are not the only groups who stress the primacy of profit maximization to an economic system. The sociologist Peter Berger has recently defended capitalism in his book *The Capitalist Revolution* (1986). His definition of capitalism emphasized the profit motive. He wrote that the most useful definition of capitalism is "production for a market by enterprising individuals or combines with the purpose of making a profit" (p. 19).

Not unexpectedly, corporate executives often explain and defend their economic decisions along similar lines. An important national newspaper has been criticized for publishing advertisements from the Kingdom of Saudi Arabia. The paid advertisements have described a large and varied number of available professional and technical positions. Critics point out that Saudi Arabia has never concealed the fact that its laws forbid women to work with men, and, indeed, women are barred from most occupations (a practice that is prohibited in the United States). In response to a suggestion that the newspaper require all advertisers to declare themselves as equal opportunity employers, an executive at the newspaper replied that it would not be acceptable to refuse advertisements just because "we might disagree with the policies pursued by the countries in which advertisements are located." He went on to state (echoing an extreme interpretation of Friedman's position) that the policy of the newspaper was that it is "improper to use an economic sanction: the declination of advertising in furtherance of our editorial view" (as quoted in *Boycott Report*, 1992).

Although Friedman's critics often attempt to paint him as a lone wolf, his views are arguably mainstream. In the introduction to his book, *New Challenges to the Role of Profit*, Benjamin Friedman suggested that the traditional view is still dominant. Accordingly, he wrote that "The standard textbook view is that firms seek to make as much profit as possible within the constraints imposed by production technology (supply factors) and market conditions (demand factors). The great preponderance of scholarly research in economics . . . either implicitly or explicitly accepts this proposition, in order to provide a guide for determining firms' behavior" (1978, p. 3).

We conclude this section with what, for the purposes of our study, is the most important implication of the traditionalist view. It can be stated in the form of a testable hypothesis as follows: Firms, which are screened on the basis of social responsibility, will be characterized as inferior investments using traditional financial statement analysis criteria. This hypothesis follows directly from Friedman's observation that social responsibility, if it means anything at all, implies that the business manager "must act in some way that is not in the interest of his employers." As stated above, however, a review of the literature is inconsistent with this hypothesis. Therefore, although Friedman's view may be both rigorous and somewhat convincing, it is apparently not descriptive in the sense that it is not supported by the available empirical evidence. We now turn to a discussion of these studies.

THE PARADOX OF SOCIAL COST: EMPIRICAL EVIDENCE

Each of the studies discussed in this section explicitly examined the statistical relationship between perceived corporate social responsibility and traditional financial performance. Appendix A briefly describes the important characteristics of these 21 studies. In this appendix we disclose the social responsibility and financial performance criteria used in each study. In addition, we briefly summarize the main results and make some additional comments.

The studies that we reviewed were published over 20 years. The first study was published in 1972 and the last in 1992. The studies used a wide variety of methodologies and variables to test for an association. For example, Belkaoui (1976) compared risk-adjusted market returns between companies that disclosed pollution control information in their annual reports, versus a control sample of non-disclosing firms during a four-month period following annual report disclosure. By contrast, Sturdivant and Ginter (1977) examined the difference in ten-year earnings per share growth between firms that scored high on a CSR reputational index and low scoring firms. Both of these studies were interested in answering the same basic research question. To what degree is CSR related to traditional financial performance? However, both studies chose different ways to measure CSR (annual report disclosure versus reputational index), different ways to measure financial performance (market returns versus a financial accounting measure), and different time horizons (four months versus ten years).

In addition to using different methodologies and variables, there also exists a wide diversity in terms of industries examined. Among the industries were chemical, electric power, food processing, iron and steel, and pulp and paper. Some of the reported studies went beyond individual industry analysis and examined interindustry effects (see, for example, Cotrill, 1990).

Finally, underscoring the interdisciplinary nature of the research question, studies have been published in numerous academic journals. Five were published in the *Academy of Management Journal*, three in *Accounting Review*, and two in *Accounting, Organizations, and Society*. The 11 remaining studies were published in different journals, ranging from *Journal of Economic Studies* to *Journal of Business Ethics*. The alternative approaches and assumptions adopted in each of the studies reflects the unique contributions of each of the academic disciplines that have participated in this research, including accounting, business ethics, economics, finance, and management. This diversity should mitigate problems associated with experimental deficiencies that might result from any one approach.

The most important observations that suggest themselves from our literature review are listed below.

1. Our single most important observation is that, of the 21 studies, 12 reported a positive association between CSR and financial performance, 1 reported a negative association, and 8 reported no measurable association. As opposed to Ullmann (1985), we conclude that there is a consistent pattern in terms of this association. While we agree with Ullmann when he wrote that "conflicting results were reported even in cases based on the same sample of firms" (p. 543), we strongly disagree with his interpre-ation that "no clear tendency can be found." Table 2.1 compares the results of our literature review to Ullmann's. Notice that, even according to Ullmann's accounting, of the 13 studies that he identified as examining the relationship between CSR and financial performance, 8 found positive correlations, 1 found negative correlations, and the remaining 4 studies reported no correlations. While it is evidently true that not all studies report that CSR firms perform better than non-CSR firms, the overwhelming preponderance of the evidence indicates that CSR firms perform at least as well as other firms. We believe that this finding directly contradicts the traditionalist view of the corporation. This surprising empirical regularity constitutes *prima facie* evidence for the existence of the "paradox of social cost." To the extent that social activities are costly to the firm (even while creating

positive externalities), one would predict a negative relationship between social performance and financial performance at the individual firm level. In the next section, we will discuss five plausible explanations to these findings.

TABLE 2.1
Corporate Social Responsibility and Traditional Financial Performance:
Summary of 21 Empirical Studies — Principal Findings

Direction of Association	1993 Results*	Ullmann (1985)†
Positive Association	12	8
Negative Association	1	1
No Association	8	4
Totals	21	13

*This column summarizes the principal findings of the 21 studies reviewed in Appendix A in this book.
†This column summarizes the principle findings of the 13 studies reviewed by Ullmann (1985).

2.   In examining CSR performance, numerous surrogates have been employed. As shown in Table 2.2, of the 21 studies, 9 used a measure of environmental performance, 6 used reputational indexes, and 2 used both disclosure and South African related criteria. Of the 12 studies that reported some positive association, there is no predominance of any one variable. Four of the nine studies that employed environmental performance as the CSR surrogate, and four of the six studies that used a reputational index, reported a positive association.

3.   In addition to using alternative measures for CSR, the studies have also employed a wide variety of measures for financial performance. Table 2.3 provides additional details. Note that 6 of the 21 studies focused solely on financial accounting returns, 7 based their results on market based returns, and still others used multiple criteria. The 12 studies that reported positive associations are not driven by any one variable. For example, three of the studies that reported positive associations were based on accounting data alone, and four were based on either market data alone or multiple criteria.

4.   The observation that researchers employed many different methodologies is corroborated by Table 2.4. Six of the studies examined CSR and financial performance of more than 61 firms, while seven of the

TABLE 2.2
Corporate Social Responsibility and Traditional Financial
Performance: Summary of 21 Empirical Studies — Corporate
Social Responsibility Criteria Used

Social Responsibility Criteria	Firms using Criteria	Firms using Criteria and Reporting Positive Association	Firms using Criteria and Reporting Negative Association
Environmental Performance	9	4	0
Reputational Index	6	4	1
CSR Disclosure	2	3	0
South African Investment	2	0	0
CEO Attitudes	1	0	0
Multiple Criteria	1	1	0
Totals	21	12	1

TABLE 2.3
Corporate Social Responsibility and Traditional
Financial Performance: Summary of 21 Empirical
Studies — Financial Performance Criteria Used

Financial Performance Criteria	Firms using Criteria	Firms using Criteria and Reporting Positive Association	Firms using Criteria and Reporting Negative Association
Stock Price Returns	7	4	0
Financial Accounting Returns	6	3	1
Market-based Measure of Risk	2	1	0
Multiple Criteria	6	4	0
Totals	21	12	1

studies included less than 20 in their sample. There are advantages and disadvantages to large and small sample studies. For example, small sample sizes may result in better estimates of CSR. Large sample sizes will minimize sample bias. Methodological diversity should mitigate problems associated with experimental deficiencies that might result from any one approach.

TABLE 2.4
Corporate Social Responsibility and Traditional
Financial Performance: Summary of 21 Empirical
Studies — Sample Size

Sample Size	Firms using Criteria	Firms using Criteria and Reporting Positive Association	Firms using Criteria and Reporting Negative Association
Less than 20	7	4	0
21–40	6	3	1
41–60	2	1	0
More than 61	6	4	0
Totals	21	12	1

To conclude this part of our discussion, we note two possible limitations in interpreting and generalizing the results. First, most of the studies were relatively short-term in nature. Only 5 of the 21 studies examined more than five years of data. The implications of this deficiency will be discussed in the next section. Second, only 6 studies examined data after 1975 (even though 13 studies were published after 1979). There exists, therefore, a need to update some of these earlier studies. Nevertheless, the body of work reviewed here represents a strong case against the traditionalist conception of CSR. Most studies to date have presented evidence that is inconsistent with the traditionalist hypothesis. We next turn to an extensive discussion of five plausible explanations to this seeming paradox.

THE PARADOX OF SOCIAL COST:
FIVE EXPLANATIONS

We will discuss five possible explanations to the empirical results presented in the previous section. The explanations should not be viewed as mutually exclusive. In fact, each explanation provides additional insight into the nature of CSR, and, thus, provides a more realistic understanding of a complex phenomenon.

Explanation 1. Socially Responsible Firms Are Identical to Non-socially Responsible Firms

As we emphasize throughout this study, the notion of socially responsible investing is often a vague and ill-defined term. It is almost impossible to provide a precise definition. Further, social responsibility is always a function of perception. Even if there is a growing consensus on a number of issues, such as environmental concern or employee relations, there is still enough disagreement that all general observations about the degree of CSR will be met with some opposition. It is, therefore, tempting to suggest that because of the uncertainty surrounding definitions of CSR there is no such thing as CSR, and, therefore, firms that may have been identified as socially responsible are, in fact, no different from other, non-socially responsible firms. If this proposition holds, then the paradox described in the previous section disappears.

There is ample anecdotal evidence that is consistent with this explanation. For example, the New York *Times* recently reported (February 11, 1993) that the Sun Oil Company of Philadelphia, the twelfth largest oil company in the United States, became the first Fortune 500 company to endorse the Valdez Principles (or at least a watered-down version in which some of the original principles were negotiated). These principles are a code of corporate environmental conduct that was devised following the 1989 Alaskan oil disaster. According to Robert H. Campbell, Sun's chairman and chief executive, there is a tremendous "philosophical congruence" (as quoted by the New York *Times*) between what Sun already does and the environmental principles. In fact, Campbell emphasized at the signing ceremony that he did not foresee any major changes in company operations. To the extent that Sun Oil's observations are generalizable to other oil companies and other industrial corporations, one should not anticipate any negative financial repercussions following the signing of the Valdez Principles.

That there may be minimal direct costs associated with CSR (relative to the size of the corporation) is suggested in a recent comment in Prudential's annual report. Robert Winters, the chief executive officer (CEO), wrote that the firm considers social responsibility "critical to our success." He further disclosed that "The Prudential Foundation gave more than $16 million to various worthy causes." The discussion about CSR in the CEO's letter consumes almost 10 percent of the total disclosures (in terms of paragraphs), whereas the $16 million charitable contribution consumes less than one-tenth of 1 percent of reported net income.

Support for the idea that there is no difference between socially responsible firms and other firms is the possibility that all major U.S. corporations who abide by the law are by definition socially responsible. Regulatory requirements and the constant threat of increased regulatory actions, coupled with an increasingly hostile tort system, may provide ample incentive for U.S. corporations to engage in socially responsible behavior. Any attempt, therefore, to distinguish between socially responsible firms and other firms is essentially arbitrary. At least in the area of pollution control, there is some evidence to support this conjecture. Shane and Spicer (1983), in studying pollution ratings produced by the CEP, stated that the council's criteria "to rate the overall efficacy of companies' pollution-control systems correspond fairly closely to legislative requirements promulgated under the Clean Air Act Amendments . . . and the Federal Water Pollution Control Act" (p. 524).

There is no doubt that in some instances CSR is nothing more than self-advertising. On the other hand, there is also no doubt that this explanation is not complete. There are often substantial costs associated with CSR behavior. For example, Freedman and Jaggi (1982) reported that in highly polluting industries as much as 20 percent of the total amount of capital expenditures has been devoted to pollution abatement. Belkaoui (1976) suggested that in the steel industry the percentage may reach as high as 25 percent.

While it is true that some of the surrogates that have been used to measure CSR are not precise, it is extremely unlikely that there are no differences between firms that are perceived as having met CSR criteria and those who are not. It is unlikely that all, or even most, of the attempts to distinguish between socially responsible firms and non-socially responsible firms have been meaningless. The ability to obtain information about socially responsible actions has become less difficult. Rockness and Williams (1988) surveyed managers of socially responsible mutual funds about sources of social information. Among the most important sources of information were the companies themselves and government agencies. In addition, private social responsibility organizations like Franklin Research and Investor Responsibility Research Center were also mentioned. In total, the authors listed 39 different sources of social information that were cited by at least one fund manager.

At the same time that CSR information has become easier to obtain, mutual funds that advertise themselves as socially responsible have begun to define the practice with more and more exactness. Table 2.5

summarizes both the positive and negative screens used by nine of the most important and influential socially responsible mutual funds. Issues like environmental concern, South Africa, weapons production, and employee relations were cited by almost all of the mutual funds examined.

TABLE 2.5
Social Responsibility Screens Used by Nine Mutual Funds

	Number of Funds using Screen
Negative Screens	
South Africa	8
Weapons	7
Nuclear power	6
Tobacco, alcohol, gambling	3
EPA violations, polluters	1
Positive Screens	
Environmental issues	8
Employee relations	6
Corporate citizenship	4
Product quality and safety	4
Alternative energy	3

Note: This table reports the number of mutual funds that explicitly cited the above social responsibility screens in the fund prospectuses. It is based on the following nine mutual funds: Calvert-Ariel Appreciation Fund, Calvert Social Investment Fund, Domini Social Index Trust, Dreyfus Third Century, New Alternatives, Parnassus Fund, Pax World Fund, Rightime Social Awareness Fund, and Schield Progressive Environmental Fund.

Source: Social Investment Forum, updated August 1991.

Therefore, if real differences exist between socially responsible firms and other firms, the original question remains. We now turn to a second plausible explanation.

Explanation 2. The Experiments to Test the Association between Corporate Social Responsibility and Traditional Financial Performance Have Not Been Carefully Designed or Controlled

According to this explanation, socially responsible firms may not be identical to non-socially responsible firms. However, the experiments to test the association between CSR and financial performance have not documented an inferior performance for CSR firms because the tests have not been well-designed.

For example, Vance (1975) argued that earlier association studies had not been validated. His main concern was that the earlier studies adopted an extremely short window to measure financial performance. Cochran and Wood (1984) noted that earlier studies (including Vance) lacked methodological rigor in the sense that they failed to measure "risk-adjusted" returns.

Ullman (1985) concluded that "studies of the relationship between social performance and economic performance are highly questionable when social disclosure is used as a proxy for social performance" (p. 545).

Cochran and Wood suggested that reputational indexes used to measure CSR are "highly subjective and thus may vary significantly from one observer to another" (p. 43). A further and, perhaps, more severe criticism is whether or not the reputational indexes are even purporting to measure CSR. For example, at least two studies have used *Fortune* magazine's annual survey of corporate reputations as the surrogate for CSR (McGuire, Sundgren, & Schneeweis, 1988; Cotrill, 1990). The appropriateness of this measure can be questioned because, of the eight key attributes respondents were queried about to determine corporate reputations, arguably, only two were directly related to issues of CSR. The eight key attributes of corporate reputation listed by *Fortune* magazine (February 8, 1993) were quality of management; financial soundness; quality of products or services; use of corporate assets; value as long-term investment; innovativeness; ability to attract, develop, and keep talented people; and community and environmental responsibility.

In addition, it has been suggested that reported results may be a function of "spurious correlations." Chen and Metcalf (1984) criticized an earlier study that documented a positive association between pollution control records and financial performance by stating that the earlier "evidence rests on spurious relationships created through one or more intervening variables. The reported significant associations might not have been observed had the effect of intervening variables been controlled (or adjusted)" (p. 168). Chen and Metcalf showed that when they controlled for size the positive association between CSR performance and financial performance is eliminated. In their words, "The results indicate that the conclusion of a moderate to strong association between pollution control record and financial indicators is not justified" (p. 174).

Roberts (1992) further suggested that, in general, many of the studies in this area are merely ad hoc attempts to relate CSR actions to selected corporate characteristics. Roberts suggested that the earlier work lacked a "theoretical foundation" (p. 610). Ullmann (1985) made a similar point when he explained that "The generally ambiguous nature of the results of the studies surveyed in the previous sections suggests that the models may be incompletely specified" (p. 551).

In spite of these important criticisms, the possibility of methodological limitations is by no means a complete explanation. As stated in the previous section, the overwhelming preponderance of evidence indicates that CSR firms perform at least as well as other firms. Examining the observations delineated above, there is no reason to believe that a systematic bias has been introduced. We, therefore, turn to a third possible explanation.

Explanation 3. A Conscious Pursuit of Corporate Social Responsibility Goals Causes Better Financial Performance

This third possibility represents an alternative view to the traditional conception of the business enterprise. It is the antithesis to Adam Smith's powerful and famous observation. In describing the capitalist, Smith wrote: "In spite of their natural selfishness and rapacity, though they mean only their own convenience, though the sole end which they proposed from the labors of all the thousands they employ, be the gratification of their own vain and insatiable desires . . . they are led by an invisible hand . . . and without intending it, without knowing it, advance the interest of society" (1937, p. 423). The prediction that social responsibility might lead to better firm performance cuts across the ideological spectrum. Variants of this position have been boldly articulated by conservative thinkers, including George Gilder, Michael Novak, and Irving Kristol; centrists, including Arthur Okun and Clarence Walton; and radical writers, including the sociologist Severyn Bruyn and economists like Samuel Bowles and Herbert Gintis. This idea has also been periodically suggested by empirical researchers and corporate executives.

In stark contrast to Adam Smith's view, George Gilder celebrated the role of the entrepreneur (1984).

Even if we do not ask economists to perform as moral philosophers, we should demand that they accurately observe the world. Observing the world, one can see scarce factual foundation for the prevailing view of entrepreneurial activity. The capitalist is not merely a dependent of capital, labor, and land; he defines and creates capital, lends value to land, and offers his own labor while giving effect to the otherwise amorphous labor of others. He is not chiefly a tool of markets but a maker of markets; not a scout of opportunities but an inventor of them; not a respondent to existing demands but an innovator who evokes demand; not chiefly a user of technology but a producer of it. He does not operate within a limited sphere of market disequilibria, marginal options, and incremental advances. For small changes, entrepreneurs are unnecessary; even a lawyer or bureaucrat would do. (p. 17)

He concluded this discussion by emphasizing, "It is the entrepreneurs who know the rules of the world and the laws of God. Thus they sustain the world. In their careers, there is little of optimizing calculation, nothing of delicate balance of markets. . . . They are the heroes of economic life" (p. 19).

Michael Novak (1982) has also criticized the traditional views. In reviewing the theories about democratic capitalism inherited from Adam Smith, Jeremy Bentham, Ludwig von Mises, Frederik von Hayek, and Milton Friedman, he wrote, "The typical mistake of classic thinkers on this subject is to have laid too small a foundation to support the lived world of democratic capitalist society as we have experienced it. They have too chastely considered the economic system in abstraction from the real world, in which the political system and the moral-cultural system also shape the texture of daily life" (p. 36). Accordingly, he described a central element of democratic capitalism, virtuous self-interest, as follows:

The laws of free economic markets are such that the real interest of individuals are best served in the long run by a systematic refusal to take short-term advantage. Apart from internal restraints, the system itself places restraints upon greed and narrowly constructed self-interest. Greed and selfishness, when they occur, are made to have their costs. A firm aware of its long-term fiduciary responsibilities must protect its investments for future generations. It must change with the time. It must maintain a reputation for reliability, integrity, and fairness. . . . Thus a firm committed to greed unleashes social forces that will sooner or later destroy it. Spasms of greed will disturb its own inner disciplines, corrupt its executives, anger its patrons, injure the morale of its workers, antagonize its suppliers and purchasers, embolden its competitors, and attract public retribution. In a free society, such spasms must be expected; they must also be opposed. (p. 93)

Among the so-called neo-conservatives, Irving Kristol has also voiced concern over the traditional view of the corporation, especially as advocated by Friedman. (See *Two Cheers For Capitalism*, 1978, pp. 63–64.) In discussing the rationale for corporate philanthropy, Kristol recognized that the only justification for corporate charity (as distinct from individual charity, which "refines and elevates the soul of the giver" [p. 134]) is that it must "serve the longer-term interests of the corporations." He continued, "Corporate philanthropy should not be, and cannot be, disinterested" (p. 134). Kristol's view is consistent with the possibility that a conscious pursuit of corporate social responsibility goals (Kristol himself used the term "social responsibility" to describe controllable philanthropic expenditures) may cause better financial performance, especially in the long run.

Arthur Okun concluded his book, *Equality and Efficiency: The Big Tradeoff*, by stating, "the market needs a place, and the market needs to be kept in its place" (1975, p. 119). Even while recognizing the limitations of a market-based system, Okun justified the profit motive along the lines we are discussing here. In defending his belief that a reliance on self-interest is not offensive as an organizing principle for the economy, he wrote that "self-interest is consistent with an enlightened selfishness that creates loyalties to family, community, and country, as institutions that benefit the individual and extend his range of interests" (p. 49).

Clarence Walton, one of the earliest proponents of CSR, similarly noted that "Corporations will be around a long time and durable organizations exist by doing things right — right in the fullest sense of the word" (1992, p. 60).

At the other end of the ideological spectrum, more radical theorists have, from time to time, also entertained the possibility that social responsibility may lead to better financial performance. Bowles and Gintis (1987) suggested that democratically controlled firms may be more efficient than the traditional corporate form of organization. This prediction is suggested by the possibility that "the change in the locus of command" that would be necessarily a part of a democratically controlled firm "may be expected to reduce the wage and surveillance costs of generating a given level of labor performed" (p. 78).

Severyn Bruyn has also predicted a positive link between social performance and economic performance. Unlike the traditional perspective, he dismissed the notion that there must be a trade-off between them, stating that the relationship between CSR and financial performance is a synergistic one. Bruyn (1987) wrote, "In reality, social considerations in the investment process can actually enhance the possibilities of economic return. The fact is that the two values are not necessarily exclusive. Social and economic values can be maximized together, and this creative synergism is the practical direction taken by social investors today" (p. 12).

The possibility that the association between CSR and financial performance may be the result of a causal relationship, as discussed here, has also been periodically suggested by empirical researchers. In presenting evidence that CSR firms in the food-processing industry outperformed non-CSR firms, Bowman and Haire (1975) explained that, while there is not a one-to-one relationship between CSR and financial performance, nevertheless, CSR is "a signal of the presence of a style of management that extends broadly across the entire business function and leads to more profitable operation" (p. 54). The authors continued that "it is exactly this ability to sense, adapt, negotiate with, and cope with these forces that is . . . the sign of managerial excellence and hence profitability" (p. 54).

Sturdivant and Ginter (1977) provided evidence that socially responsible firms (as measured by a reputational index) outperformed a control sample in terms of ten-year earnings per share growth. They elaborated: "It would appear that a case can be made for an association between responsiveness to social issues and the ability to respond effectively to traditional business challenges. . . . A company management group which reflects rather narrow and rigid views of social change and rising expectations might also be expected to respond less creatively and effectively in the traditional but also dynamic arenas in which business functions. Hence there is the stronger economic performance" (p. 38).

Kahneman, Knetsch, and Thaler (1986) have provided survey evidence that supports the causal link between CSR and financial performance. They argued that a realistic description of our economic system must include the fact that consumers, suppliers, and employees care about being treated fairly and treating others fairly. In addition, they are willing to resist unfair firms even at a positive cost to themselves. Satisfying the fairness constraint may lead to better long-run financial performance.

Corporate executives also have noted the connection between CSR and financial performance. For example, Thornton Bradshaw (see Jones, 1982), the CEO of the Radio Corporation of America, recently wrote, "Those who believe, as I do, in the intrinsic value of the decentralized market system must act now to develop a more humanistic, responsible, and innovative form of capitalism to meet society's demands as well as satisfying its needs" (p. 151).

Executives have attempted to describe the connection between CSR and financial performance through the vehicle of the annual report. For example, the president of Ben and Jerry's Homemade Ice Cream, Inc. recently defended his commitment to a social agenda in his president's letter to shareholders as follows:

We have a two-part bottom line. This Annual Report presents both our financial progress and our progress in contributing to the quality of life in our communities. . . . We believe that if we focus on the quality of everything we do, the traditional business measures will fall into place. We are master ice cream and frozen dessert makers. We want to be a force for progressive social change. And our staff is perpetually enthusiastic about our future. If we can continue to grow these values as fast as we grow the company we'll be fine. (*Annual Report*, 1989)

In summary, the view discussed here is a powerful countervailing paradigm to the traditional view of the corporation. Further, it is apparently more consistent with the available empirical evidence than the alternative view. Nevertheless, there are major limitations. First, it is highly doubtful whether the variables that have been used as surrogates for CSR in the empirical studies are always closely related to the notions of social responsibility that have been emphasized by Gilder, Novak, Okun, and even Bowles and Ginter. As emphasized in the introduction, CSR is part economic philosophy and part political philosophy. While there is a clear overlap between CSR as it has developed in practice over the last 20 years and the notions of responsibility as discussed in this section, the overlap is not exact. Therefore, the explanation offered here may not be entirely appropriate for the empirical findings previously reported.

Second, intuitively, the explanation is not completely compelling. Simply put, if doing good is always costless, why is not everyone good? By the logic offered here, even a scoundrel would eventually notice that it is in his or her best interest to choose CSR. We, therefore, need a view that can explain the persistence of scoundrels as well as saints.

Finally, the explanation as stated here is too general. In Explanation 5, below, its scope is limited. First, however, we discuss the following alternative explanation.

Explanation 4. Only Firms that Perform Better in Terms of Financial Criteria Can Afford a Conscious Pursuit of Corporate Social Responsibility Goals

Social responsibility does not cause enhanced financial performance; rather, financial performance allows for the performance of discretionary social actions. Anecdotal evidence supports this view. For example, in response to poor financial performance, firms with "no layoff" policies have been forced to shrink their employee base. What was once viewed as a permanent part of corporate strategy to meet CSR goals is no longer economically viable.

According to this view, especially as it has been articulated by Ullmann (1985), the motivation for engaging in socially responsible actions is external to the corporation. Ullmann suggested that social performance should be viewed as a result of a "strategy for dealing with stakeholder demands" (p. 552). He continued, "When stakeholders control resources critical to the organization, the company is likely to respond in a way that satisfies the demands of the stakeholders."

A central component to Ullmann's stakeholder model is the link between financial performance and social responsibility. In Ullmann's view, economic performance is posited as an independent variable. Therefore, economic performance explains CSR, not vice versa. "Economic performance determines the relative weight of a social demand and the attention it receives from top decision makers. In periods of low profitability and in situations of high debt, economic demands will have priority over social demands. . . . Economic performance influences the financial capability to undertake costly programs related to social demands" (p. 553).

McGuire, Sundgren, and Schneeweis (1988), following Ullmann, concluded their empirical study by noting that "Firms with high performance and low risk may be better able to afford to act in a socially responsible manner" (p. 869). Echoing Ullmann, they continued, "In essence, it may be more fruitful to consider financial performance as a variable influencing social responsibility than the reverse."

Chen and Metcalf (1984), examining the relationship between pollution control and financial performance, similarly suggested that "economically, a firm with high earnings is more likely to incur pollution abatement costs than one with low earnings" (p. 173).

More recently, Roberts (1992), in presenting empirical evidence that is consistent with Ullmann's stakeholder model, concurred that it is economic performance that leads to higher levels of CSR, and not the other way around. "The importance placed on meeting social responsibility goals may be secondary to meeting the economic demands that impact directly on a company's continued viability. Economic performance directly affects the financial capability to institute social responsibility programs. Therefore, given certain levels of stakeholder power and strategic posture, the better the economic performance of a company the greater its social responsibility activity and disclosures" (p. 599).

Ullmann's stakeholder model is consistent with the traditional view of the corporation in the sense that both view social responsibility as a net cost to the corporation. In addition, a benefit of the stakeholder model is that it is compatible with much of the empirical evidence that was reviewed above.

This approach represents an important development in understanding the nature of CSR. Effective managers need to satisfy all important stakeholders, not simply the demands of shareholders. Further, it is plausible to assume that meeting the needs of consumer groups, environmental activists, labor unions, the government, and other stakeholders is becoming more important to corporate managers. Nevertheless, it may not be accurate to suggest that the demands for social responsibility are always external to the corporation, as the stakeholder model implies.

An important and unappreciated implication to the stakeholder model is that if there is a net cost to CSR, in the long run it should be detected. In other words, firms that start out with a financial advantage and can, therefore, afford to engage in socially responsible actions should over time (assuming they continue to engage in CSR) forfeit their financial advantage. That CSR activities represent a material cost is directly suggested in Ullmann's observation quoted above that economic performance influences the financial capability to undertake costly programs related to social demands. This testable implication of the stakeholder model has never been formally examined. Therefore, one of the main goals of the current research is to examine the long run financial performance of a group of socially responsible firms.

Explanation 5. Sometimes, a Conscious Pursuit of Corporate Social Responsibility Goals Causes Better Financial Performance

Explanation 3, as suggested above, is too extreme. Explanation 5 limits its applicability. According to this last explanation, there are two types of socially responsible actions. Some social actions have no net costs, and, in fact, may benefit the firm in the long run, while other socially responsible actions (even while creating positive externalities) are costly to the firm. This explanation suggests that the traditional view and Explanation 4 are wrong in assuming that social actions do not benefit the firm. The position adopted here proposes that Friedman's statement that the very term "social responsibility" must imply behavior that is not in the interest of the corporation is needlessly provocative (see Friedman, 1970, p. 33). Our disagreement with Friedman is a definitional one. Friedman's view is that any action that benefits the firm is, by definition, not socially responsible. Alternatively, we suggest that whether or not an action benefits the firm (in terms of increased financial performance) is irrelevant to its classification as socially responsible.

If Explanation 5 is to help unravel the paradox of social cost, we must add the plausible assumption that the major corporations that have been studied in the empirical literature and are perceived as being socially responsible are pursuing corporate goals that are consistent with financial performance goals. Corporate management, on average, rejects those activities that are not congruent with shareholder demands. Under this assumption, we do not anticipate a negative association between CSR and financial performance.

The possible existence of two types of social actions, although intuitively appealing, has received little attention. The important advantages of this explanation are that

it is consistent with the empirical studies examined above,

it does not assume that the motivation for CSR is always external to the firm (as in Explanation 4), and

it is consistent with the views of corporate executives and board members.

The explanation offered here is based, in part, on Peter Drucker's (1989) definition of CSR. In his book *The New Realities*, Drucker wrote: "We know in rough outline the social responsibility of the pluralist institutions of society. We know that their first social responsibility is to do their job. We know secondly that they have responsibility for their impacts — on people, on the community, on society in general. And finally we know that they act irresponsibly if they go beyond the impacts necessary for them to do their own job, whether it is taking care of the sick, producing goods, or advancing learning" (p. 86). In describing the responsibility for organizational impacts, Drucker stated:

It has to exercise considerable control over the people who work for it; otherwise, it cannot do its job. It has considerable impact on people who are customers whether they buy a company's goods or are patients in a hospital. And it has impacts on bystanders. The factory that closes at four-thirty in the afternoon creates a traffic jam for everyone in the community. Responsibility for one's impacts is the oldest principle of the law. It does not matter whether the institution is at fault or is negligent. The Roman lawyers who first formulated this principle called it the "doctrine of the wild animal." If the lion gets out of its cage, its keeper is responsible. Whether the lion's keeper was careless and left open the door of the cage, or whether an earthquake released the lock, is irrelevant. (pp. 87-88)

Drucker's "doctrine of the wild animal," thus, insures that the "institution has a duty — but also a self-interest — to limit its impact to what is actually needed for the discharge of its social function" (p. 88).

  Drucker distinguished among different areas of social responsibility. With regard to community responsibility, he wrote that "It must fit the institution's competence. It must fit its value system. It must be an extension of what it is doing rather than a diversion" (p. 92). Similarly, he discussed political responsibility. "Unless institutions learn, however, to ask what the community requires, they will increasingly lose public support" (p. 94). In addition, he emphasized, "Political responsibility is thus the self-interest of the pluralist institution" (p. 94). Writing about employee relations, Drucker contended that the organization's increasing dependence on the "knowledge worker" will lead to a redefinition of the rights and responsibilities of the employee. "To deprive anyone of his or her job — or diminish it — the institution must act according to pre-set standards, especially standards of performance" (p. 95).

  According to Drucker, social responsibility is a necessary ingredient to long-term financial health. That this is true is illustrated by the following example:

In the early years of this century a Chicago clothing merchant, Julius Rosenwald, took over an ailing mail-order house called Sears, Roebuck. Within ten years it had become the world's largest and most profitable retailer. One reason was Rosenwald's recognition that to prosper, Sears needed a healthy farm community. But the American farmer at the beginning of the century was in desperate straits, dirt-poor, isolated, backward in his technology, with little access to education and even less to modern farming methods. Yet there was an enormous amount of agricultural technology available, the result of well over a hundred years of research and experimentation. Rosenwald invented the Farm Agent to act as the change agent on the American farm. He financed this new institution himself for ten years until it had become so successful that the U.S. government took it over. By then the farmer had acquired enough competence and purchasing power to buy from Sears. Milton Friedman, had he been consulted, would have told Rosenwald to stick to business and leave concern for the farmer to the government. In other words, community responsibility that is concern for a healthy and viable community is not "philanthropy" for the pluralist institution. It is self-interest. (pp. 91–92)

Consistent with Explanation 5, Drucker also underscored the existence of two types of socially responsible actions. He pointed out that social responsibility is effective only under stringent conditions. It must fit the organization's value system. "It must be an extension of what it is doing rather than a diversion" (p. 92). In a recent article, Drucker (1992) continued on the theme of social responsibility. He wrote that "we had better be watchful because good intentions are not always socially responsible. It is irresponsible for an organization to accept — let alone pursue — responsibilities that would impede its capacity to perform its main task and mission or to act where it has no competence" (p. 99).

In addition to Drucker, a number of attempts have been made to distinguish between socially responsible actions that lead to better financial performance and those that do not. It is often assumed that there may be a link between pollution control and financial performance. For example, in discussing the compatibility between high levels of pollution control and high profit levels, Bragdon and Marlin (1972) suggested that the poor performance of the domestic steel industry must be viewed as a consequence of poor management. They believed that "good managements are likely both to earn higher profits and to be more careful in protecting the environment" (p. 10). According to their view, while Japanese and European firms were investing in new equipment with lower pollution levels, U.S. steel companies refused to change over to the new technology. That foreign companies have outperformed domestic steel producers is in part a "reflection of lower costs associated with better pollution control" (p. 9).

Coffey and Fryxell (1991), in suggesting that CSR involves taking actions pursuant to obligations beyond the economic and legal sphere, isolated four components of CSR that may lead to better firm performance. "Evidence of corporate social responsiveness may be related to a broad range of issues including: pollution abatement, product safety, advertising messages, the role of women and minorities in the firm. That the capability to change with the social climate is important for long-term economic performance is a basic tenet of strategic management" (p. 439).

A major limitation to Explanation 4 is its insistence that the motivation for CSR is always external to the organization. This observation is plainly seen in Ullmann's prediction that firms with poor economic performance, low stakeholder power, and a passive strategic posture are not likely to engage in CSR (p. 553). Explanation 5, however, predicts that even in a period of poor economic performance, a corporation may find it in its own interest to pursue CSR objectives. The motivation for CSR can, thus, be an internal decision to increase long-term financial performance while simultaneously meeting responsibilities for corporate impacts.

Cornell and Shapiro (1987) further explored this possibility. What are the advantages to the shareholder of honoring product warranties beyond legal requirements? Cornell and Shapiro suggested that what motivates corporate executives to honor implicit contracts (with no legal ramifications) is that executives believe that the long-term value of the firm is a direct function of its ability to sell not only explicit claims but also implicit claims. In the authors' words, the market value of a corporation includes "organizational capital which equals market value of all future implicit claims the firm expects to sell" (p. 10).

To clarify the distinction between implicit and explicit claims, the authors used the following example. IBM priced the PC_{jr} to include

Both the price of the hardware and the prices of the implicit claims for future support, software, product enhancements, and the like. As it became clear that PC_{jr}'s success in the market was limited, IBM faced a difficult decision. If the company chose to discontinue the product line it would clearly lessen the organization liabilities connected with PC_{jr}. On the other hand, discontinuing the product reduces the payout on implicit claims previously issued by the company, which in turn reduces the firm's organizational capital by causing the prices of future implicit claims to fall. (p. 9)

The problem that IBM and other corporations face is that if they fail to honor implicit claims for one product, stakeholders will rationally assume that they are less likely to honor implicit claims for other products, including items yet to be marketed. "For firms such as IBM that choose to identify all their products with the company name, the spillover effect is likely to be particularly strong" (p. 9).

In this example, IBM chose what we might label the socially responsible solution. The company chose to discontinue the production of the PC_{jr}, but it also undertook a major advertising campaign to let PC_{jr} owners and other stakeholders know that "If you own a PC_{jr} you can be sure it is still a well-cared for member of the IBM PC family" (p. 10). They chose this solution, not out of a sense of altruism, but because of concern with their long-term financial performance.

By contrast, when Exxon phased out its office systems division, it "provided minimal support for customers and other stakeholders of that division" (p. 9). Presumably, Exxon executives perceived little spillover effect as a result of this decision, because the office systems division was incidental to their main line of business.

Cornell and Shapiro extended their analysis beyond customer warranties. They wrote: "When a firm hires a new employee, he or she frequently receives promises about the work environment, the evaluation process and the opportunity for advancement, as well as an explicit employment contract. . . . In a similar fashion, implicit claims are sold to stakeholders, such as suppliers and independent firms that provide repair services and manufacture supporting products" (pp. 6–7).

If Explanation 5 holds, and if we add the plausible assumption that the major corporations choose, on average, to pursue those CSR goals consistent with financial goals, in the long run, socially responsible firms may actually outperform non-socially responsible firms in terms of traditional financial performance. This is the most important implication of Explanation 5. Firms that have been identified as socially responsible should maintain or even increase their relative financial advantage over non-socially responsible firms.[3] This implication is in direct opposition to the implication of Explanation 4. As we pointed out, this implies that firms that start out with a financial advantage, and can, therefore, afford to engage in socially responsible actions, should, over time (assuming they continue to engage in CSR), forfeit their financial advantage.

NOTES

1. The relationship between CSR and the law is interesting, complex, and, generally speaking, beyond the scope of this study. Nevertheless, we consider two important questions. First, to what extent can a money manager use social criteria in allocating funds? Second, to what extent can the board of directors pursue CSR objectives?

According to Bruyn (1987, pp. 8–9), the legal arguments constraining money managers' use of social responsibility criteria originated out of an 1830 ruling by a Massachusetts court in *Harvard College* v. *Amory*. The argument offered there was as follows: "All that can be required of a trustee to invest is, that he shall conduct himself faithfully and exercise a sound discretion. He is to observe how men of prudence, discretion and intelligence manage their own affairs, not in regard to speculation, but in regard to permanent disposition of their funds, considering probable income, as well as the probable safety of the capital to be invested." This decision was interpreted to imply that trustees must be guided primarily by the economic interests of the beneficiaries and the safety of their capital. However, Bruyn continued, when beneficiaries claim that social criteria should be used the law requires that it is permissible and even mandatory to apply social screens. Exceptions have been made to the so-called prudent man rule in the following two cases: *Blankenship* v. *Boyle* and *Withers* v. *Teachers Retirement System of the City of New York*. Under certain circumstances, therefore, "social investment can be made properly without penalty" (Bruyn, 1987, p. 10). Nevertheless, Bruyn concluded, "Clearly, there are some legal risks."

The question of whether the board of directors can use CSR criteria in formulating policy has been discussed at length by Jay Lorsch (1989). In trying to explain why directors do not explicitly discuss the true purpose of the board, Lorsch wrote:

It appears that, in many boards, a group norm has evolved prohibiting such discussion. The core of the inhibition is the widely held view that directors' legal responsibility is solely to shareholders. If directors believe this, discussing other accountabilities seems unnecessary and, if not illegal, at least, inappropriate. The vast majority of directors seem unaware that the legal context defining their accountability is changing, both apropos of the normal conduct of corporate affairs and the relation to directors' actions in considering a sale of a company. The most obvious source of change is innovation in the laws of the seventeen states "which permit directors to consider the interests of constituents other than corporation's shareholders." (p. 50)

To the extent that CSR activities benefit stakeholders other than shareholders, it is unclear, at least to directors, precisely what the law allows.

2.   Having spelled out what we believe is an unbiased view of Friedman's writings, it should be pointed out that even his "unequivocal" argument is ambiguous enough to provide some sanction for corporate management to engage in what they might view as socially responsible actions. For example, in describing the proper role for corporate executives, Friedman has written that their responsibility is to conduct the business in accordance with the desires of stockholders, "which generally will be to make as much money as possible while conforming to the basic rules of the society, both those embodied in law and those embodied in ethical custom" (1970, p. 33). Although he certainly does not accept the term "social responsibility," even Friedman recognizes the existence of corporate obligations beyond mere legal requirements. Even corporate managers of the Friedman type need to make moral decisions about ethical custom and cannot escape formulating an answer to Friedman's rhetorical question: "If businessmen do have social responsibility other than maximizing profits for stockholders, how are they to know what it is?" (1962, p. 133). Is this question different in kind from the idea that if businessmen need to conform to the basic rules of society, which include those embodied in ethical custom, how are they to know what they are?

In his book (with Rose Friedman, 1980) the author further elaborated:

Narrow preoccupation with the economic market has led to a narrow interpretation of self-interest as myopic selfishness, as exclusive concern with immediate material rewards. Economics has been berated for allegedly drawing far-reaching conclusions from a wholly unrealistic "economic man" who is little more than a calculating machine, responding only to monetary stimuli. That is a great mistake. Self-interest is not myopic selfishness. It is whatever it is that interests the participants, whatever they value, whatever goals they pursue. (p. 18)

3.   Our point here is that CSR may cause better long run financial performance. We also recognize, however, that firms experiencing extreme financial distress may cut back first on CSR programs. In this special case, a deteriorating financial performance may directly lead to fewer CSR activities. This is true because there are fewer legal requirements associated with CSR commitments (implicit claims) than other, more traditional, corporate activities (explicit claims). It may be less costly to break CSR commitments than other, more formal, contractual agreements.

3

The Association between Corporate Social Responsibility and Financial Performance: Methodology and Results

A major goal of the first phase of the study is to explore the association between corporate social responsibility (CSR) and traditional financial performance. In this way, we can begin to distinguish between explanations 4 and 5 discussed in the previous section.

CREATING THE SAMPLE

In particular, we examine the long-term financial performance of 53 firms that have been identified by the Council on Economic Priorities (CEP) as being socially responsible (Group 1) and compare their performance to a control sample matched by both industry and size (Group 2). In addition, to test for changes over time, we compare the relative performance of groups 1 and 2 in two time periods (1985–87 and 1989–91). A listing of the 106 firms selected for our study is included in Appendix B.

The CEP described the companies in Group 1 as ethical portfolio companies. In selecting these firms the CEP "drew both on the holdings listed in the prospectuses of the socially responsible mutual funds and on lists provided by SIF" (p. 19). Additional information was drawn from reports prepared by Franklin Research and Development and Clean Yield. There are several advantages of choosing the CEP firms for our study.

First, the CEP is highly regarded as a credible source of information on CSR. Numerous published studies have used previous CEP studies as the basis for forming measures of CSR. For example, of the 21 studies we reviewed in the previous chapter, 5 used CEP studies. We concur with Shane and Spicer (1983), who concluded that "The most detailed, consistent, and comparable data bearing on corporate social performance has been published by the CEP. It appears to be the most active external producer of information in this area" (p. 522).

Second, the CEP ratings are not unique. The firms included in Group 1 tend to be rated high in terms of CSR by numerous external groups. Table 3.1 summarizes some characteristics of the groups 1 and 2 firms and provides additional support to the CEP ratings. There is significant overlap between the Group 1 firms, as identified by the CEP, and firms included in the Domini 400 Social Index. Of the 53 firms identified by the CEP as ethical, 44 firms are included in the Domini Index. Only 12 of the Group 2 firms were included in the Domini Index. About half of the Group 1 firms (24 firms) were rated among the "100 Best Companies to Work For," while only 2 of the Group 2 firms were included on this list. Further, 12 of the Group 1 firms were among the "75 Best Companies for Working Mothers." None of the Group 2 firms were identified on this list.

TABLE 3.1
Characteristics of Group 1 and Group 2 Firms

Characteristics	Group 1		Group 2	
	Number	Percent	Number	Percent
Domini 400 Social Index	44	83	12	23
100 best companies to work for	24	45	2	4
75 best companies for working mothers	12	23	0	0
50 best places for blacks to work	12	23	0	0
Best companies for women (50)	8	15	1	2
More than 20 percent employee ownership	4	8	0	0
Top 100 Defense Department contractors	3	6	1	2
Direct investment in South Africa	2	4	6	11
Top 50 manufacturers releasing toxic chemicals	1	2	1	2
Top 100 nuclear weapons contractors	0	0	1	2
Tobacco companies	0	0	1	2

Table 3.1 also indicates that few of the Group 1 firms are listed among the "Top 100 Defense Department Contractors" or the "Top 50

Manufacturers Releasing Toxic Chemicals." Finally, and not surprisingly, none of the Group 1 firms were included among the "Top 100 Nuclear Weapons Contractors" or were identified as tobacco companies.

To achieve the goals of this study we needed an aggregate measure of CSR, as opposed to a measure of one or more of the components of CSR. The CEP ratings, based on an assessment of 12 specific CSR components, provided a convenient and well-respected third-party assessment. Further, we believe that the CEP ratings provide a more precise measure of CSR than those obtained from the next best competitor, *Fortune* magazine's annual survey of corporate reputations. As discussed in the previous section, the appropriateness of the survey results can be questioned given that, of the eight key attributes respondents were queried about to determine corporate reputations, arguably, only two were directly related to issues of CSR.

The Group 1 firms were selected from diverse industries, thus enhancing the generalizability of the results. Table 3.2 reveals that 21 industries

TABLE 3.2
Industry Classifications for Socially Responsible Firms

SIC Codes	Industry Classification	Number of Firms
2000–2099	Food and kindred products	9
2300–2399	Apparel and other finished products	2
2500–2599	Furniture and fixtures	1
2600–2699	Paper and allied products	1
2700–2799	Printing, publishing, and allied products	3
2800–2899	Chemicals and allied products	9
3000–3099	Rubber and miscellaneous plastic products	1
3100–3199	Leather and leather products	1
3500–3599	Industrial, commercial machinery, computer equipment	4
3600–3699	Electrical, other electrical equipment, except computers	3
3700–3799	Transportation equipment	1
3800–3899	Measuring Instruments, photo goods, watches	3
4500–4599	Transportation by air	3
4800–4899	Communication	1
4900–4999	Electric, gas, and sanitary services	3
5300–5399	General merchandise stores	3
5600–5699	Apparel and accessory stores	1
6500–6599	Real estate	1
7300–7399	Business services	1
7500–7599	Auto repair, services, parking	1
7900–7999	Amusement and recreation services	1

are represented among the 53 Group 1 firms. Nine firms were selected from both Food and Kindred Products (SIC codes 2000–2099) and Chemicals and Allied Products (SIC codes 2800–2899). Eleven industries had just one member among the Group 1 firms. The relatively large proportion of firms in Food and Kindred Products and Chemical categories might be considered *prima facie* evidence of an industry effect. The possibility that there exists an association between perceived social responsibility and industry has been documented by Cotrill (1990) and Bowman and Haire (1975).

Many of the 53 firms in Group 1 have been described as socially responsible by a wide variety of outside evaluators. The CEP is one of the most highly regarded external producers of social responsibility information. The 53 firms represent a diverse sample of companies. The sample, thus, provides an important and inherently interesting point of departure.

FINANCIAL PERFORMANCE CRITERIA

We compared firm characteristics between Groups 1 and 2 over a broad range of traditional financial variables. The variables fall into one of four major categories. Specifically, we examined:

1. Market-based measures of performance, including market return, price to earning ratio, and market value to book value;
2. Accounting-based measures of performance, including return on assets, return on equity, and earnings per share;
3. Measures of risk, including current ratio, quick ratio, debt to equity ratio, interest coverage, Altman's Z-score,[1] and market beta; and
4. Other firm-specific characteristics, including capital investment intensity, size, number of lines of business, and dividend-payout ratio.

In all, we examined and reported results for 16 traditional financial statement variables. Each of the variables is constructed from data available on COMPUSTAT. (COMPUSTAT is a machine-readable data base with historical financial information for over 1,500 publicly traded corporations.) Individual year mean and median results are displayed in tables 3.3, 3.4, 3.5, and 3.6.

In general, our results indicate that there is little evidence that the Group 1 firms can be characterized as inferior investments relative to the Group 2 firms. This finding, once again, contradicts the traditionalist hypothesis. In addition, some evidence exists that supports the stronger proposition that the Group 1 firms can be characterized as superior investments relative to Group 2 firms.

Market-based Measures of Performance

According to Table 3.3, the market returns for Group 1 were slightly better than the market returns for Group 2. The overall means for the seven-year period were 13.57 percent and 11.54 percent, respectively. Further, in four of the seven years the Group 1 firms had higher returns than Group 2 firms. In 1986, Group 1 outperformed Group 2 firms at the 10 percent level of significance, and in 1988 this relationship was reversed.

TABLE 3.3
Market-based Measures of Performance
Group 1 versus Group 2, 1985–91

	1985	1986	1987	1988	1989	1990	1991	Mean
Market returns								
G1 mean	24.96	16.01*	–3.87	4.18*	21.69	–0.30	32.33	13.57
G1 median	33.25	12.80	–4.10	2.50	25.20	–7.40	26.50	12.68
G2 mean	26.69	5.15	3.19	15.97	16.48	–11.10	24.39	11.54
G2 median	32.70	13.00	–0.50	15.10	18.10	–17.60	22.00	11.83
P/E ratio								
G1 mean	19.52	21.06	18.78	15.08	20.59	19.91*	24.43	19.91
G1 median	15.79	17.48	14.94	13.57	17.59	15.69	20.99	16.58
G2 mean	23.07	22.72	20.63	16.29	22.30	15.68	22.87	20.51
G2 median	17.16	17.73	15.35	13.45	14.96	13.47	18.85	15.85
Market to book value								
G1 mean	2.94	2.99	3.20	3.00	3.39**	2.90	3.67**	3.16
G1 median	2.29	2.28	2.65	2.61	3.06	2.39	2.79	2.58
G2 mean	3.30	3.37	2.84	2.56	2.96	2.70	3.02	2.96
G2 median	1.97	2.79	2.09	2.23	2.18	1.76	1.94	2.14

*10% Level of Significance
**5% Level of Significance

There was almost no difference between the price to earning ratios for the two groups. The overall mean for Group 1 firms was 19.91 for the seven-year period, compared to 20.51 for the Group 2 firms. The only year in which there was a statistically significant difference at the 10 percent level was 1990, when the price to earning ratios were 19.91 and 15.68, favoring the Group 1 firms.

Among the market-based measures, the most consistent results were related to the market value to book value ratios. This ratio relates the market capitalization of the firm to the accounting valuations. The overall means for the seven-year period were 3.16 versus 2.96 for groups 1 and 2, respectively. From 1987 through 1991, Group 1 firms had a higher ratio in each year. In 1989 and 1991, the differences were significant at the 5 percent level.

Accounting-based Measures of Performance

Table 3.4 presents the accounting-based measures of performance. These results are similar to the market-based results in indicating either no difference or a slight advantage to the socially responsible firms.

TABLE 3.4
Accounting-based Measures of Performance
Group 1 versus Group 2, 1985–91

	1985	1986	1987	1988	1989	1990	1991	Mean
Return on assets								
G1 mean	7.54	6.01	8.55**	8.23	7.98*	6.91	6.69	7.42
G1 median	6.55	6.30	8.00	6.70	7.10	6.20	6.45	6.76
G2 mean	5.99	7.70	6.67	7.10	6.07	6.23	4.81	6.37
G2 median	6.15	6.60	6.90	7.00	6.70	6.60	5.15	6.44
Return on common equity								
G1 mean	16.53	14.28	19.45**	19.86	19.93	16.81	15.89	17.54
G1 median	15.35	15.30	18.80	19.60	18.30	16.50	15.70	17.08
G2 mean	14.04	17.68	15.50	17.39	17.70	40.63	15.93	19.84
G2 median	15.80	18.10	15.70	16.90	16.60	15.20	11.80	15.73
EPS								
G1 mean	3.14	2.29	2.55	2.45	2.61	1.96	1.60	2.37
G1 median	2.69	2.22	2.20	2.46	1.90	2.14	2.12	2.25
G2 mean	3.08	2.35	2.36	2.49	2.43	2.00	1.45	2.31
G2 median	3.09	1.96	2.13	2.20	2.30	2.05	1.43	2.17

**5% Level of Significance
*10% Level of Significance

The first variable presented in Table 3.4 is return on assets. It has been suggested that return on assets "takes the particular set of environmental factors and strategic choices made by a firm as given and focuses on the profitability of operations relative to the investments (assets) in place" (Stickney, 1990, p. 161). An important characteristic of this accounting measure is that it separates financing activities from both operating and investing activities. The overall means for the seven-year period were 7.42 percent and 6.37 percent, for groups 1 and 2, respectively. In two of the seven years, 1987 and 1989, the Group 1 firms had a significantly higher return on assets. In 1987, the mean for the Group 1 firms was 8.55 percent, versus 6.67 percent for the Group 2 firms. Similarly, in 1989 the mean for the Group 1 firms was 7.98 percent, versus 6.07 percent for the Group 2 firms. Only in 1986 did the Group 2 firms outperform the Group 1 firms, and this difference was not statistically significant. We conclude from these results that the Group 1 firms were certainly no less efficient in generating income from assets in place than the Group 2 firms and, in fact, were slightly more efficient.

Although return on common equity is usually highly correlated with return on assets, it is useful to report this variable as an additional measure of financial performance. It has been argued that return on common equity, which relates income available to common shareholders to average amount of common equity in use during a period, should be emphasized as the appropriate tool for assessing the profitability "from the viewpoint of an investor in a firm's common stock" (Stickney, 1990, p. 219). Not surprisingly, the results here also indicate a slight advantage to the Group 1 firms. Although the overall means for the seven-year period were slightly higher for the Group 2 firms, this result was primarily driven by the 1990 results, which must be interpreted with care. Notice that in 1990, although the return on common equity for Group 2 was apparently much higher than the Group 1 results, the difference is not significant, and, in fact, Group 1 had a higher median. The difference in the reported means between groups 1 and 2 is the result of statistical outliers in Group 2. The only significant difference was 1987, in which the Group 1 firms had a mean of 19.45 percent, versus Group 2's mean of 15.50 percent.

The last variable included in Table 3.4 is earnings per share. The overall means for the seven-year period were $2.37/share versus $2.31/share for groups 1 and 2, respectively. Although the Group 1 firms outperformed the Group 2 firms in four of the seven years, in none of the years were the results significant, even at the 10 percent level.

Measures of Risk

Table 3.5 presents results related to traditional measures of risk. The first two variables presented in the table, the current ratio and the quick ratio, provide an assessment of the corporations' ability to meet their short-term obligations as they come due. These measures are often labelled short-term liquidity ratios. For both the current ratio and the quick ratio, the overall means for the seven-year period were nearly identical. For the current ratio the Group 1 mean was 1.92, and the Group 2 mean was 1.91. Similarly, for the quick ratio the Group 1 mean was 1.13, and the Group 2 mean was 1.10. The only significant difference (at the 10 percent level) was for the current ratio in 1987. The Group 1 mean was 1.87, which was higher and, thus, slightly less risky, than Group 2's mean of 1.62.

In addition to examining short-term liquidity ratios, Table 3.5 summarizes results for three long-term solvency measures: interest coverage, debt to equity ratio, and Altman's Z-score. Each of these measures indicates the firms' ability to meet interest payments and principal payments as they come due.

First, for the interest coverage variable, the overall means for the seven-year period were slightly higher (less risky) for the socially responsible firms. For the Group 1 firms the mean was 7.77, and for the Group 2 firms the mean was 6.77. (These numbers show that for every $1 of interest expense there was, on average, $7.77 and $6.77, respectively, of income before interest expense and income taxes.) In 1987, the difference between the two groups was significant at the 5 percent level; Group 1 was 9.19, and Group 2 was 6.40. Further, in every year from 1987 through 1991, Group 1 had higher interest coverage than Group 2 in terms of both means and medians.

Second, with respect to the debt to equity ratio, which measures the amount of long-term debt financing in a firm's capital structure, although there is some indication that the socially responsible firms may be more risky, these results should not be overstated. Although the overall mean for the seven-year period is higher for the Group 1 firms than for the Group 2 firms, this result is, in part, a function of statistical outliers among the Group 1 firms. In fact, the mean of the median results for the entire seven-year period, which is unaffected by the outliers and arguably more relevant for our purposes, is nearly identical between groups 1 and 2. The means of the median results for the seven-year period were 45.28 percent and 44.06 percent, respectively. Further, in none of the individual

TABLE 3.5
Measures of Risk, 1985–91

	1985	1986	1987	1988	1989	1990	1991	Mean
Current ratio								
G1 mean	2.09	2.02	1.96	1.85	1.85	1.87*	1.79	1.92
G1 median	1.86	1.91	1.86	1.77	1.85	1.77	1.67	1.81
G2 mean	2.14	1.87	1.97	1.99	1.99	1.62	1.77	1.91
G2 median	1.91	1.55	1.73	1.67	1.59	1.43	1.40	1.61
Quick ratio								
G1 mean	1.30	1.14	1.22	1.07	1.08	1.08	1.04	1.13
G1 median	1.15	1.04	0.99	0.96	0.99	0.93	0.89	0.99
G2 mean	1.21	1.17	1.13	1.15	1.11	0.90	1.01	1.10
G2 median	1.10	0.90	1.00	1.00	0.95	0.75	0.78	0.93
Debt/equity ratio								
G1 mean	61.29	75.30	78.79	106.57	139.40	229.43	315.75	143.79
G1 median	33.71	29.89	36.77	39.77	60.92	61.27	54.61	45.28
G2 mean	76.69	74.93	68.39	93.89	95.05	121.78	147.12	96.84
G2 median	40.28	39.98	48.43	41.75	52.20	45.02	40.76	44.06
Interest coverage								
G1 mean	7.81	7.38	9.19**	8.43	7.54	6.41	7.63	7.77
G1 median	4.14	4.78	5.72	4.52	3.60	3.43	3.74	4.28
G2 mean	9.30	8.80	6.40	6.02	5.50	5.52	5.82	6.77
G2 median	4.12	4.77	4.18	4.03	3.34	3.21	3.19	3.83
Altman's Z-score								
G1 mean	10.46	10.08	12.27	13.56	20.61	17.31	19.37	14.81
G1 median	8.12	7.26	7.19	5.89	5.49	5.22	6.24	6.49
G2 mean	10.91	9.87	12.97	13.68	10.22	14.37	15.20	12.46
G2 median	5.99	4.68	5.53	5.40	5.08	5.60	6.02	5.47
Market beta								
G1 mean	1.17*	1.15	1.17*	1.14	1.15	1.14	1.17*	1.16
G1 median	1.20	1.30	1.20	1.10	1.10	1.20	1.20	1.19
G2 mean	1.04	1.06	1.04	1.06	1.07	1.09	1.04	1.06
G2 median	1.10	1.10	1.10	1.20	1.20	1.10	1.10	1.13

*10% Level of Significance
**5% Level of Significance

years were the differences between the two groups statistically significant.

Altman's Z-score, a weighted average of five financial statement ratios, has been found useful in predicting bankruptcy. It, thus, captures a different dimension of corporate risk. In interpreting the Z-score, the lower the outcome, the greater the probability of bankruptcy. The results summarized in Table 3.5 indicate that, in five of the seven years, the Group 1 firms had higher Z-scores than the Group 2 firms. Focusing on the median results, in all seven years Group 1 scored higher than Group 2. The overall mean results for the seven-year period were 14.81 and 12.46, respectively.

The last variable examined in Table 3.5 is market beta. This variable compares the variability of stock returns for a given company with the variability of the stock market as a whole. Higher levels of beta indicate more stock market variability in relation to the market. It is the only one of the 16 variables examined that consistently favored the Group 2 firms. Once again, however, the differences should not be overstated. The overall mean results indicate that the Group 1 betas (overall mean 1.16) are about 9 percent higher than the betas for Group 2 (overall mean 1.06). Focusing on the individual year results, in each year the Group 1 firms had higher betas than the Group 2 firms. In three years — 1985, 1987, and 1991 — these differences were significant at the 10 percent level.

Other Firm-specific Characteristics

In addition to examining the performance and risk measures discussed above, Table 3.6 reports comparative statistics for four additional variables: capital investment intensity, total assets, number of lines of business, and dividend-payout ratio.

The capital investment intensity variable was created by deflating new capital investments each year by total assets. The results show that the Group 1 firms had higher investment ratios in all but one of the seven years. In fact, in 1985, 1987, and 1988, the capital investment intensity variable is significantly higher (at the 5 percent level) for the Group 1 firms than it is for the Group 2 firms. The ratio for Group 1 was 11 percent, 10 percent, and 10 percent, respectively, for 1985, 1987, and 1988, compared to 9 percent, 7 percent, and 8 percent for Group 2. The overall means for the seven-year period are consistent with these findings.

In addition to greater investment activity, the Group 1 firms are larger than the Group 2 firms in terms of total assets. These results are interesting and important. By 1991, as seen in Table 3.6, the mean asset size of Group 1 firms was over $6 billion, compared to a mean asset size of over $4 billion for Group 2 firms. Although the disparity is mitigated

TABLE 3.6
Other Firm-specific Characteristics, 1985–91

	1985	1986	1987	1988	1989	1990	1991	Mean
Capital investments/assets								
G1 mean	0.11**	0.09	0.10**	0.10**	0.09	0.09	0.08	0.09
G1 median	0.09	0.06	0.08	0.08	0.08	0.08	0.07	0.08
G2 mean	0.09	0.10	0.07	0.08	0.08	0.08	0.07	0.08
G2 median	0.08	0.09	0.05	0.07	0.07	0.06	0.06	0.07
Total assets								
G1 mean	3,040.60*	2,870.02	3,647.38*	4,809.14*	5,240.85**	5,413.71*	6,267.24*	4,469.85
G1 median	1,715.56	2,140.20	2,019.36	2,460.40	2,743.90	2,975.71	3,254.84	2,472.85
G2 mean	2,358.00	3,366.32	2,949.88	3,112.53	3,449.99	4,243.84	4,228.39	3,386.99
G2 median	1,555.26	1,879.12	1,896.30	1,793.80	1,971.60	2,149.62	2,027.39	1,896.16
Lines of business								
G1 mean	NA	2.35	2.02	2.21	2.17	2.08	2.14	2.16
G1 median	NA	2.00	1.00	2.00	1.00	1.00	1.00	1.33
G2 mean	NA	2.02	2.20	2.08	2.02	2.02	2.02	2.06
G2 median	NA	1.50	2.00	2.00	2.00	2.00	2.00	1.92
Dividend payout ratio								
G1 mean	48.70	41.15	40.35	35.66	45.69	44.94	56.52	44.72
G1 median	37.96	32.50	34.73	33.61	36.86	40.65	41.74	36.86
G2 mean	54.20	50.42	40.79	32.07	35.09	35.36	48.07	42.29
G2 median	39.26	38.91	27.19	26.34	29.73	33.68	33.28	32.63

*10% Level of Significance
**5% Level of Significance

somewhat in focusing on median results rather than mean results, the difference is statistically significant at the 10 percent level.

The differences in terms of size between the two groups is somewhat surprising. This is especially true because our strategy in creating the control sample was to select firms as close as possible in terms of asset size. In some cases, however, this strategy did not result in extremely close matches. Table 3.7 illustrates the difficulty. According to the table, about 40 percent of the firms in Group 1 were the biggest firms in their respective industries, ranked on the basis of total assets. For example, Group 1 includes K-Mart and Johnson & Johnson. These are the number one firms in the variety stores industry and the pharmaceutical preparation industry, respectively. Because the socially responsible firms were so big, many of the control firms, by construction, had to be smaller than their socially responsible counterparts.

TABLE 3.7
Distribution of Industry Rankings of Socially Screened Firms

Ranking	Number of Firms	Percentage of Firms
1	21	40
2	10	19
3	4	8
4	2	4
5	5	9
6	3	6
7	3	6
more than 8	5	9
Total	53	100

Note: This table displays the number and percentage of socially screened firms that were the largest firm in the industry, the second largest firm, etc.

This size effect confirms results of previous research. For example, Trotman and Bradley (1981) concluded that companies that provide social responsibility information are, on average, larger in size than companies that do not disclose this information. Arlow and Gannon (1982), in reviewing the literature, suggested that social responsiveness might be linked to such factors as industry and organizational size. Finally, McGuire, Sundgren, and Schneeweis (1988), using *Fortune*

magazine's annual survey of corporate reputations, concluded that total
assets were positively linked to social responsibility reputations.

Returning to Table 3.6, it is interesting to note that even given the substantial size differences between groups 1 and 2, there are no statistically
significant differences between the groups in terms of number of lines of
business. This is true, even though for five of the six years (data were not
available for 1985) Group 1 had a higher mean than Group 2.

Similarly, there were no significant differences for the last variable
examined, the dividend payout ratio, even though Group 1 had higher
means from 1988 through 1991. The overall seven-year means were
44.72 percent and 42.29 percent for groups 1 and 2, respectively.

AN EXAMINATION OF TIME TRENDS

In addition to comparing the performance of groups 1 and 2 over the
entire seven-year period, we also tested for changes over time.
Specifically, we compared the relative performance of groups 1 and 2 in
two time periods (1985–87 and 1989–91).

To assess the relative performance, we first divided the sample into
two time periods, an early and late period. Next, for the early period, we
compared the three-year means for each of the 16 variables between
groups 1 and 2. We repeated the procedure for the late period. Table 3.8
lists those variables in which there were statistically significant
differences in one time period, but not the other.

Our analysis shows that, in terms of the market-based measures of
performance, risk measures, and other firm-specific characteristics, there
is no evidence that the Group 2 firms performed better relative to the
Group 1 firms in the later period than in the earlier period. The single
piece of evidence supporting the enhanced performance of the Group 2
firms in the later period is one of the three accounting-based measures of
performance, return on common equity. There was no relative
improvement for either return on assets or earnings per share. Thus, most
of our data is inconsistent with Explanation 4, which posits a net cost
associated with social responsibility actions.

By contrast, the preponderance of evidence is that Group 1 firms
performed relatively better than Group 2 firms in the later period. This is
especially true for the market-based measures of performance. As
indicated in Table 3.8, the market returns for the Group 1 firms were
nearly twice as high in the later period than the market returns for the
Group 2 firms. Similarly, the mean of the market value to book value in
the later period is significantly higher for the Group 1 firms. Notice also

TABLE 3.8
Trend Analysis

	Early Period Means 1985–87	Late Period Means 1989–91
Market returns		
G1	10.29	17.85*
G2	16.04	9.85
P/E ratio		
G1	20.48*	23.50
G2	23.15	23.07
Market to book value		
G1	3.18	3.32*
G2	3.03	2.90
Return on common equity		
G1	17.99**	18.33
G2	14.83	24.83
Interest coverage		
G1	8.50	7.65**
G2	8.16	5.47
Capital investments/assets		
G1	.10**	.09
G2	.08	.08
Total assets		
G1	3,366.36	5,608.93**
G2	2,684.18	3,949.48

*10% Level of Significance
**5% Level of Significance

Note: This table lists each of the 16 variables in which there was a statistically significant difference (at either the 5 percent or 10 percent level) between Group 1 and Group 2 in one time period, but not the other.

that in the early period the price to earnings ratio favored Group 2, but the effect reverses in the later period. All three of these findings indicate a relatively enhanced performance of the socially responsible firms in the later period.

In addition to improvements in market-based measures of performance, our results also indicate a relative improvement in one of the risk measures. The interest coverage ratio, which is not significantly different between the two groups in the early period, is significantly higher (less risky) for Group 1 in the later period. None of the other risk measures indicate any changes over time.

Finally, examining other firm-specific characteristics, Table 3.8 shows that, although there is no significant difference in terms of size in the early period between the two groups, in the later period the socially responsible firms are significantly larger than the control sample. The only other variable that showed changes over time was the dividend payout ratio. In the late period, Group 1 paid out a significantly higher proportion of net income as dividend payments.

To summarize the results of this section, most of the variables showed either no change between the two time periods or indicated an improved performance over time for the socially responsible firms relative to the control sample. It is certainly premature to conclude that, in general, socially responsible firms perform better over time.

The issues involved in assessing socially responsible actions and measuring financial performance are too complex and nuanced to expect definitive answers. However, based on our results to date and to the extent they are corroborated by additional studies using alternative samples and even longer testing periods, Explanation 5 becomes more plausible. Explanation 5 suggested that some CSR activities might cause better financial performance. A relative improvement in the performance of socially responsible firms over time is consistent with this hypothesis.

The tone of our discussion and the formulation of the conclusions to our empirical work are purposely tentative. This underscores the exploratory nature of the research project. Nevertheless, the consistency of the results reported here and the persistent finding across numerous studies that socially responsible firms certainly perform no worse and, perhaps, perform better than non-socially responsible firms is an important and intriguing finding that demands additional attention. Although our understanding of the relationship between CSR and traditional financial performance is not complete, in the next chapters we extend our empirical analysis by examining the relationship between social responsibility and information disclosure.

NOTE

1.   The Altman's Z-score has been found useful in predicting bankruptcy. It is actually a combination of five additional financial ratios. For a full discussion see Stickney (1990) or Altman (1968).

II

THE LANGUAGE OF CORPORATE SOCIAL RESPONSIBILITY

Language frames how we look at things, what concepts we employ to describe and analyze them, and how we react emotionally. One of the problems with much of traditional management and, for that matter, modern economics is that it is filled with Taylorist language — words and terms that denigrate the capacities and motives of employees and presuppose a conflictual relationship. In this regard, the quality movement offers much-improved language. It is a powerful call to action.

Pfeffer, 1994, pp. 214–215

4

Annual Reports as a Medium for Voluntarily Signalling and Justifying Corporate Social Responsibility Activities

The purpose of this phase of the study is to investigate and measure annual report disclosures of social responsibility activities for a sample of firms that had previously been identified as meeting corporate social responsibility (CSR) criteria. The companies were identified by the Council on Economic Priorities (CEP). We compare these results to an analysis of social responsibility disclosures for a control sample.

One way of succinctly articulating the goal of this study is as follows: Do socially responsible firms "signal" their identity through the annual report? That is, are socially responsible firms more likely than other firms to communicate information about corporate socially responsible goals and activities to their shareholders? In addition, where the answer to the first question is yes, we also ask whether or not management provides a formal justification, using strategic or non-strategic language, for its selection of socially responsible activities. Specifically, we analyze the text of the president's letter to shareholders, through the use of content analysis, for any differences between articulated goals and disclosures of specific activities related to CSR.

There are numerous reasons for examining the president's letter to shareholders. First, the letter is systematically made available to all shareholders and other interested parties. The president's letter is a highly visible document that is available on an annual basis. Second, it is not difficult to understand. In a recent survey of individual investors' readership and use of the annual report, Epstein and Pava (1993) concluded that the president's letter to shareholders was the least difficult item to understand. Third, the letter is specifically targeted to share-holders (although this is not universally the case). This is important, given that our research focus is primarily concerned with how managers disclose and justify CSR activities to shareholders. Finally, and perhaps most importantly, the president's letter provides an open-ended and relatively unrestricted medium for managers to voluntarily convey information to interested parties. While this is also true for the man-agement, discussion, and analysis section of the annual report (MD&A) (Pava and Epstein, 1993), our initial comparison between CSR dis-closures in the MD&A and the president's letter strongly indicated man-agement's propensity to convey CSR information through the president's letter rather than the MD&A. Wolfe (1991) similarly concluded that the management discussion focused solely on technical explanation of financial results, and reference to CSR issues was absent.

ALTERNATIVE PERSPECTIVES AND HYPOTHESES

A number of different theoretical perspectives have been developed with regard to the issue of CSR. Many of these alternative perspectives imply different predictions concerning the amount and kinds of disclosures and the degree of association between CSR disclosures and CSR performance. In this section, we examine four major hypotheses: No Disclosure, No Association, Positive Association, and Full Dis-closure. In the following discussions we explicitly articulate the four distinct hypotheses and discuss the perspectives and assumptions that give rise to them.

No Disclosure: No Meaningful Disclosure about Corporate Social Responsibility Activities Exists

Corporations have no incentive to report to shareholders any activities related to CSR. Two assumptions underlie this perspective.

First, investors are assumed to attach value exclusively to the expec-tation of future cash flow and not to the creation of positive or negative externalities. Engel (1979) has described this as "the presumptive share-holder desire to maximize profit" (p. 3). Second, the perspective assumes that there is a negative association between CSR activities and financial performance. Thus, it is assumed that higher levels of CSR activities lead to lower levels of financial performance. These two assumptions, taken together, lead to the strong conclusion that companies rated high in terms of CSR, in an environment that allows for strictly voluntary disclosures, will have significant incentives in place not to disclose this information, especially through the president's letter to shareholders. In addition, companies rated low in terms of CSR would be indifferent to this type of disclosure, and would not have much to report, in any case.

Abbott and Monsen (1979) have summarized and defended this hypothesis as follows: "There are theoretical reasons to expect the corporation to under report its social involvement activities. Since social involvement activities are also costs, reading of such social activities by shareholders can be taken to mean that the firm's management is failing to put highest priority on the interests of the shareholders by not maximizing income available to be distributed as dividends" (p. 506).

According to this view, it is highly unlikely that the president of the company will report to shareholders his or her decision to cut environmental pollution below expected legal requirements. In fact, reporting disclosures of social responsibility activities would be no more likely than the reporting of the purchase of a corporate jet strictly for personal use. Spicer (1978b) described this view as the "classical view." He wrote that, according to the classical view, "the criteria for judging performance of a business firm are strictly economic. It follows that the set of components of corporate social performance is empty." If, indeed, the classical view is correct, one would expect little or no disclosure about CSR activities.

No Association: Although Some Disclosures about Corporate Social Responsibility Activities Exist, There Is No Association between Actual Corporate Social Responsibility Performance and Corporate Social Responsibility Disclosures

This hypothesis has recently been articulated by Cowen, Ferreri, and Parker (1987). The authors wrote: "A company may be highly involved in social responsibility actions but may not choose to disclose such actions in the annual reports. Conversely, some companies may have little concern with societal welfare but may make numerous disclosures of relatively trivial activities to enhance their corporate image" (p. 121).

The clearest explication of this view has been offered by George J. Benston in a controversial and thought-provoking article entitled "Accounting and Corporate Accountability" (1982). Benston, applying arguments borrowed from the efficient market school, suggested that managers possess little or no latitude in terms of choosing CSR activities.

To build his case, Benston explicitly asserted (as in the classical view) that consumers, shareholders, and management demonstrate little or no demand for CSR activities. With regard to consumers, Benston described them as follows: "consumers care only for the benefits that they get from the things they purchase" (p. 90). It is, thus, asserted that consumers are not only rational in the technical sense that they maximize their own utility but also not allowed to incorporate the utility of others into their own utility calculations. With regard to shareholders, Benston's assumptions are equally limiting and one dimensional. In fact, Benston implicitly equates CSR activities to using "resources in ways that do not benefit the shareholders" (p. 89). It is certainly plausible, however, that many shareholders might possess a desire for CSR activities. We will return to this point shortly. Finally, Benston explicitly asserts that managers who are skilled at operating a company tend not to be interested in CSR activities.

Given these restrictive assumptions, Benston builds a strong analytical case suggesting the impossibility for the existence of substantial CSR activities. Benston lists four general reasons why managers are limited in terms of their choices: the market for goods and services, the markets for finance and for corporate control, the market for managerial services, and, finally, internal and external monitoring systems.

Given that Benston's consumers are rarely interested in CSR activities, the market for goods and services serves to constrain managerial decisions. Managers are unable to expend additional resources on environmental projects and pass along the costs of the CSR activities to consumers. Consumers simply will not pay more to help defray the costs of environmental clean-up.

Similarly, because shareholders put no value on CSR activities, the markets for finance and corporate control also limit the ability of managers to engage in CSR activities. Benston asserts that the "poor stewardship" associated with decisions to engage in socially responsible activities will inevitably lead to lower share prices. In turn, "the decline in the market price of corporations' shares increases the likelihood of a corporate takeover to displace the managers" (p. 91). Therefore, managers concerned about their own jobs have a strong built-in incentive to avoid CSR activities.

The market for managerial services also constrains managers. At this point, Benston equates CSR activities to "self-serving decisions" (p. 91). Thus, the more a manager is perceived as one who engages in CSR activities, the more difficult he or she will find obtaining a new managerial position. In Benston's words, "As is the case in markets generally, other producers as well as consumers have incentive to learn about and provide information on the value of the product" (p. 91). To the extent that a manager is known as a CSR manager, his or her value will decline.

Finally, and according to Benston most importantly, the existence of internal and external monitoring systems will prevent managers from "misusing the shareholders' resources" (p. 92). According to Benston, most managers (like consumers and shareholders) have no desire to engage in CSR activities. Managers, thus, find it in their own interest to set up and design internal and external monitoring systems to attest to the fact that they are not engaging in unprofitable activities like CSR. In the absence of external auditors, for example, managements' "compensation would be reduced by the amount of resources that they would be expected to divert from the shareholders" (p. 92). Simply put, it is in the interest of managers to hire auditors to attest to the fact that no CSR activity has been undertaken.

Benston's conclusion is clearly stated. Managers have little or no discretion to act other than in the interests of shareholders. Because it has been assumed that shareholders have no taste for CSR activities, managers cannot and will not engage in these activities. As part of the empirical evidence to support his position, Benston concludes this part of the discussion by prematurely noting the virtual failure of three mutual funds that were created to invest in corporations using CSR screens.

At this point, it would seem that Benston's view is closely associated with the first hypothesis above. Benston, however, is well aware of the existence of some CSR disclosures, and, therefore, must explain the phenomenon in light of his efficient market view.

To explain CSR disclosures, Benston introduces the notion of pressure groups into the analysis. Benston suggests that CSR disclosure is an attempt to mitigate "the costs that pressure groups might be able to impose" (p. 99). Managers strategically disclose selected bits of information that serve the interests of the corporation by pacifying the various pressure groups concerned with employee, consumer, and government issues. Benston continues that, because measuring CSR activities is a subjective process, it is no surprise that the reports generally favor the companies. Benston believes that, even in a regulatory environment that required CSR disclosures, the best we could hope for would be reports about social responsibility that would "have little chance of being other than public relations or other self-serving exercises" (p. 100).

Benston's position is similar to the classical view in that he concludes real CSR activity is a virtual impossibility. Nevertheless, companies have an incentive to portray themselves as if they are socially responsible. It is the "homage which vice pays to virtue" (Lindsay, 1962, p. 97). The difference between Benston and the pure classical view is Benston's explicit assumption about the existence of pressure groups. These pressure groups represent the single class of stakeholders with a demand for socially responsible actions.

Ullmann (1979) understands CSR disclosures in Germany as a result of managers trying to preempt union demands for increased wages. It, thus, provides a clear example of Benston's self-serving disclosures. Ullmann describes the German reporting environment as follows:

Today CSR is capable of serving a very different strategic purpose within the context of a drastically changed economic environment, namely to prevent demands for high wage increases. In periods of slow economic growth and unemployment, distribution conflicts intensify, corporate social reports which indicate that the largest share of the wealth created by corporations is already going to employees, can facilitate management arguments in discussion with labor unions. As the Federation of German Employers' Associations pointed out, CSR "can help reduce utopian concepts and to harmonize the social demands with the true capacity of the economy." (p. 127)

Benston's suggestion that disclosure decisions are the result of self-serving calculations on the part of managers can certainly explain many of the reporting failures documented in the national media. For example, the New York *Times* (December 17, 1993) recently gave front-page coverage to the indictment of Con Edison and two retired officials for allegedly concealing information that an explosion released large amounts of asbestos into a highly populated area of Manhattan. According to the article, following the explosion the company gave assurances that the blast did not result in the release of asbestos. On the basis of this allegedly false information, residents returned to their apartments. It is certainly plausible that Con Edison management made the disclosure decision as a result of an informal or implicit cost benefit analysis. Management at the time of the explosion may have believed it was in their interest, at least in the short run, to convey assurances to residents that all was normal.

Similarly, the following episode, as described by the New York *Times* (July 11, 1993), also suggests a strong element of strategic behavior on the part of management: "For New York and the 8.2 million people insured by Empire, questions remain. Federal and local law-enforcement agencies are investigating two sets of books kept by Empire over the last several years. Empire officials acknowledged that they supplied false financial data to the New York State Insurance Department, and used the data in their successful lobbying campaign for changes in insurance law to shore up Empire's finances."

The common thread in both of these cases is an attitude on the part of management that information can be manipulated in such a way as to further either individual or corporate goals, or both simultaneously. In each case management allegedly failed to disclose information in an open and neutral manner.

Neither of these cases is unique. Therefore, an approach like Benston's, which explicitly recognizes managers' disclosure decisions as "self-serving," possesses great intuitive appeal.[1,2] Nevertheless, we believe it is open to a number of severe criticisms. First, the argument hinges on some seemingly restrictive assumptions. Consumers, shareholders, and even managers are assumed to be indifferent toward social responsibility. While these extreme assertions may be true, Benston's empirical evidence is less than convincing. Second, the analysis leaves unanswered the question of why pressure groups (who apparently do value CSR activities) are satisfied with social responsibility reports that are merely self-serving documents. If the author of the model is aware that CSR reports are nothing more than public relations, why are pressure groups not aware of this? Analytically, it is not satisfying to conclude that the author of the model has information that some of the assumed economic players are missing. Third, the theory itself is somewhat over-advertised. It is by no means a dramatic conclusion that social responsibility reports will be self-serving, given the starting position that assumes all managerial activity is self-serving.

Yet, in spite of our reservations, Benston's paper undoubtedly provides the clearest model and the most precise statement of the assumptions underpinning this hypothesis. It, therefore, represents an important contribution to understanding CSR disclosures.

Before closing our discussion of this hypothesis, it is interesting to examine a more extreme variant of it. This variant is termed Disclosure of Negative Externalities, and states that firms disclose information concerning the imposition and transfer of costs (externalities) to non-contracting third parties.

On the face of it, this seems to be an extremely odd hypothesis. Under what conditions would managers ever disclose information about activities where the corporation successfully transferred its own costs to non-contracting third parties?

Benston, for example, explicitly dismisses this possibility. He writes, "It would be a form of self-destruction (or masochism) for corporate officers to report voluntarily that they had polluted a river or discriminated against minorities" (pp. 98–99).

Benston's conclusion deserves careful scrutiny. This is especially true because he is one of the few researchers who explicitly describes the benefits accruing to the firm if it, indeed, can successfully transfer internal costs to third parties. In fact, given the assumptions of Benston's model, there are strong incentives in place for managers to seek out creative and original strategies to transfer corporate costs to third parties. In the highly competitive environments that Benston posits, and in situations where the law is silent and pressure groups are ignorant, there are strong incentives (in the absence of any internal social responsibility constraints) for managers to invent new ways to reduce their own costs by shifting them to the public at large.

Benston's own words are worth quoting. He writes, "It benefits anyone, including the owners of corporations, to impose negative externalities on non-contracting parties." If this assumption is true, managers should own up to and unhesitatingly disclose their cost-shifting behavior. Further, if the assumptions of the model are correct, shareholders themselves should demand disclosure of this kind of behavior, as this variant hypothesis suggests. Benston knows that it is occurring, managers and shareholders know that it is occurring, so disclose it. Nevertheless, Benston concludes that such disclosures would not be beneficial to the shareholders; it is a form of self-destruction. But why?

The answer apparently lies in the inherent power of pressure groups. Although not spelled out explicitly, Benston assumes that pressure groups in possession of this information would be able to exert enormous sanctions against a corporation. Pressure groups, according to Benston, would literally be able to destroy the firm.

We believe that, although this position is not completely illogical, it is an unlikely description. We agree with Benston that disclosure of this type of activity would have extremely negative effects on the corporation. We also concur that pressure groups would use this information to attack the firm. However, we believe that the primary reason this hypothesis is not a serious consideration is the likelihood that shareholders, consumers, and most managers would view the imposition of significant corporate costs on non-contracting third parties as unethical. In other words, in addition to pressure groups, in some situations shareholders, consumers, and managers would be willing to incur costs to promote CSR goals.

For example, during the 1950s, Richardson-Merrell began developing and testing a new drug, MER/29, which they hoped would help reduce cholesterol. According to Christopher D. Stone (1975), in his book *Where the Law Ends*,

While its top officers were enthusing about the drug, and preparing for a major marketing campaign, other parts of the organization were receiving bad news. In one laboratory test all the female rats on a high dosage died within six weeks. In a subsequent test, all rats on a somewhat lower dosage had to be destroyed halfway though the experiment. On autopsy, it was revealed that they had suffered abnormal blood changes. Corneal opacities were observed in other animals. Monkeys suffered blood changes and weight loss. . . . When the company finally filed a new drug application with the FDA, seeking permission to place MER/29 on the market, its application contained many false statements. (p. 54)

Stone further suggests that, regardless of the perceived benefits to the corporation of falsifying the data, "It is hard to believe that a representative sampling of board members, fully informed of what was happening to animals in Richardson-Merrell's laboratories, would have voted to push ahead with MER/29." In explaining his view, Stone suggests that not to have done so would have run counter to "moral views that are held by the general public and general business community" (p. 135). We believe Stone is correct in assuming that the general business community might view some activities as immoral, even when they lead to greater profitability.

We conclude our discussion of this variant hypothesis by noting that virtually no one accepts it. We disagree, however, with the reasoning put forth by Benston. A simpler, more realistic, and more convincing explanation is that shareholders do not want managers to advance corporate interests by merely shifting costs to non-contracting third parties. This explanation leads us to the third hypothesis.

Positive Association: Corporate Social Responsibility Disclosures Exist. Further, There Is a Positive Association between Actual Corporate Social Responsibility Performance and Corporate Social Responsibility Disclosures

According to a recent study by Wolfe (1991), one of the most important issues concerning annual reports is whether variations in annual report disclosures are simply reflections of variations of communication of espoused values and behaviors or variations of values and behaviors in use. This hypothesis maintains the latter view.

This hypothesis suggests that firms might signal their identity as socially responsible companies through the annual report. It does not imply a one-to-one correspondence between CSR performance and CSR disclosures. It merely states that, on average, companies that are perceived as having met CSR criteria will be more likely to report this information in the annual report.

Observers agree that CSR disclosure in the United States is predominately voluntary. Wolfe describes the disclosure environment: "Though considerable resources have been spent debating and studying it, social reporting the United States remains predominately voluntary . . . and is expected to remain so. The SEC considers that social information falls outside of its area of responsibility, unless it has material economic consequences" (p. 290).

Given this voluntary environment, why would one expect this hypothesis to hold? Gibbins, Richardson, and Waterhouse (1990), in their study on the management of corporate disclosures, concluded that, among executives involved in making disclosure decisions, the credibility of the disclosures is of primary concern. Basing their conclusions on extensive interviews with corporate managers in Canadian corporations, the authors wrote, "Credibility seems central to effective disclosure. While credibility may be enhanced, for example, by employing external agents to attest to information, it also rests on the firm's disclosure reputation" (p. 138). To the extent that Gibbins, Richardson, and Waterhouse have drawn the correct conclusion from their data, they provide a strong *a priori* reason to believe that, even in the area of CSR, managers cannot afford to be perceived as manipulating disclosures merely to serve their own ends. If shareholders believe that corporate disclosures are merely self-serving attempts to manage a hostile environment, the credibility of the disclosures will soon come into question.

The hypothesis states that a positive association characterizes the relationship between CSR performance and disclosures. The two most important assumptions upon which the hypothesis is based are as follows:

1. Managers attempt to communicate information to users in a neutral and unbiased way.

2. Unlike the classical view and Benston's view, shareholders, consumers, and managers believe that some CSR activity is desirable and, therefore, real CSR activity exists.[3]

The first assumption concerning the communication of neutral information to users is a bedrock concept in accounting. According to the Financial Accounting Standards Board's (FASB) Concept Project (1980), corporate executives must satisfy their obligation to report all information that is of sufficient importance to influence the judgement and decisions of an informed user. More specifically, the FASB has warned that "the primary concern should be the relevance and reliability of the information that results." In addition, the FASB explains, "Accounting information must report economic activity as faithfully as possible, without coloring the image it communicates for purpose of influencing behavior in *some particular direction*" (emphasis in original). This well-known criterion is called neutrality.

While the second assumption above remains somewhat controversial, an increasing number of observers accept it. For example, Anderson and Frankle (1980) concluded their empirical study, "Thus the 'ethical investor' may exist and, in fact, dominate the market. Whether this finding can be attributed to altruistic or economic motivations on the part of investors has not yet been resolved" (p. 477). Similarly, survey studies of investors such as Epstein and Pava (1992) have suggested that although the stereotype is that shareholders are worried only about profits, this is clearly not the case. For example, when investors were asked to rank their preferences as to how corporate funds were to be allocated, pollution and product safety were ranked higher than dividends.

Numerous researchers have speculated about the degree of association between CSR disclosures and actual performance and have provided reasoning similar to that offered here.

Bowman (1984), in defending his use of CSR disclosure as a surrogate for actual CSR performance, wrote that he would not expect "unusual puffery" on issues like CSR. Because annual reports are written "essentially to shareholders" (p. 63), it is unlikely that managers will invent or exaggerate CSR activities.

Similarly, Wolfe believes that, in spite of its voluntary nature, there are pressures on management to report honestly and accurately. According to Wolfe, "Increased public scrutiny, competitive forces, the independent financial press, audits and antifraud laws, potential impacts on public confidence, and moral obligation motivate corporate managers to provide honest annual report information" (p. 290).

Abbott and Monsen (1979) agree that there are good reasons to believe that managers will disclose CSR activities in an unbiased and honest way. Their emphasis lies less in the perceived altruism of shareholders or Wolfe's "moral obligations" than in the need for managers to legitimate the business enterprise. According to Abbott and Monsen, "Stockholders have a vested interest in the stability and legitimacy of the entrepreneurial institution and the autonomy of that institution from state control. Aware, then, of the criticisms that have been made of the corporation, reading of its progressive views on social responsibilities in the annual report can enhance confidence of the politically savvy shareholder in managements' policies" (p. 506). Fair and honest disclosure of CSR activities might, thus, preempt government intrusion and safeguard the autonomy of corporate managers.

Full Disclosure: There Is a Positive Association between Actual Corporate Social Responsibility Performance and Corporate Social Responsibility Disclosures. Further, Some Managers Fully Articulate Corporate Goals and Justify Corporate Social Responsibility Activities in Non-strategic Terms

Not only is there a positive association between CSR performance and disclosures, but some managers will defend CSR activities by using non-strategic language in the annual report. In other words, firms engaging in CSR activities claim to do so not only to serve the financial interests of shareholders by maximizing profits but also to meet the legitimate moral and ethical claims of other stakeholder groups. This hypothesis, which of course is more extreme than the Positive Association hypothesis, has received virtually no attention in the literature on CSR disclosures. This is surprising.

For the purposes of this study, we utilize Kenneth E. Goodpaster's (1991) distinction between strategic and non-strategic decision making. According to Goodpaster:

A management team, for example, might be careful to take positive and (especially) negative stakeholder effects into account for no other reason than that offended stakeholders might resist or retaliate (e.g., through political action or opposition to necessary regulatory clearances). It might not be *ethical* concern for the stakeholders that motivates and guides such analysis, so much as concern about potential impediments to the achievement of strategic objectives. Thus positive and negative effects on relatively powerless stakeholders may be ignored or discounted. (p. 57)

Management adopting a strategic perspective views all groups other than stockholder groups "instrumentally, as factors potentially affecting the overarching goal of optimizing stockholder interests" (p. 58). Goodpaster believes that weighing stakeholder considerations as potential sources of goodwill or retaliation as a practical matter "is morally neutral" (p. 57). Expanding on this point, Goodpaster continues, "The point is simply that while there is nothing necessarily wrong with strategic reasoning about the consequences of one's actions for others, the kind of concern exhibited should not be confused with what most people regard as moral concern" (p. 60).

An excellent example of strategic decision-making in the area of CSR is the decision of Wal-Mart Stores, Inc. to stop selling handguns in its stores, a move hailed by gun control advocates (Wal-Mart will continue to sell handguns by catalog). As the *Wall Street Journal* (December 23, 1993) noted, this decision "coincides with the recent heightening of the nation's long-running debate over guns and violence. The controversy has been fueled by a spate of multiple shootings and the passage of the Brady Bill, which mandates a five-day waiting period for handgun purchases." A spokesman for Wal-Mart carefully, and no doubt purposely, explained the decision purely in strategic terms. According to the spokesman, Don Shinkle, "A majority of our customers tell us they would prefer not to shop in a retail store that sells handguns." The firm makes no moral or ethical claims. Wal-Mart, at least in this instance, would prefer that this decision be understood purely in terms of cost benefit analysis. Wal-Mart apparently would like to avoid making any kind of moral or ethical stand on a visceral and hotly debated public issue.

By contrast, non-strategic decision making explicitly incorporates the legitimate rights of even the least powerful stakeholders. Goodpaster suggests that "Moral concern would avoid injury or unfairness to those affected by one's actions because it is wrong, regardless of the retaliatory potential of the aggrieved parties" (p. 60).

Is there any evidence that public companies defend corporate activities through the use of non-strategic language as the Full Disclosure hypothesis predicts? Goodpaster quotes the following memo from the chief executive officer (CEO) of a major public company to middle management. The purpose of the memo was to explain and justify the firm's decision to put significant resources behind their affirmative action program. The CEO's letter reads in part:

I am often asked why this is such a high priority at our company. There is, of course, the obvious answer that it is in our best interest to seek out and employ good people in all sectors of our society. And there is the answer that enlightened self-interest tells us that more and more of the younger people, whom we must attract as future employees, choose companies by their social records as much as by their business prospects. *But the one overriding reason for this emphasis is because it is right.* Because this company has always set for itself the objective of assuming social as well as business obligations. Because that's the kind of company we have been. And with your participation, that's the kind of company we'll continue to be. (p. 65, emphasis in original)

This memo provides an unusually stark example of what is meant by non-strategic decision making; it contrasts sharply with the Wal-Mart example. The CEO articulates an unambiguous justification of the firm's affirmative action program. The CEO implies that, even in the absence of financial gains to the corporation, the corporation has obligations to society at large. The CEO explicitly recognizes both business obligations, as well as overriding social obligations.

Based on the preceding discussions of the four hypotheses, a fairly simple model suggests itself. The degree of association between CSR disclosures and CSR performance is a function of basic assumptions about the nature of CSR activities and the nature of corporate disclosures. Table 4.1 summarizes the arguments thus far.

TABLE 4.1
Assumptions Underlying Alternative Hypotheses

	CSR Activities Exist	*No CSR Activities Exist*
Neutral disclosure	Hypotheses 3 or 4	Hypothesis 1
Self-serving disclosure		Hypothesis 2

Hypothesis 1 — No Disclosure: No meaningful disclosure about CSR activities exists.
Hypothesis 2 — No Association: Although some disclosures about CSR activities exist, there is no association between actual CSR performance and CSR disclosures.
Hypothesis 3 — Positive Association: CSR disclosures exist. Further, there is a positive association between actual CSR performance and CSR disclosures.
Hypothesis 4 — Full Disclosure: There is a positive association between actual CSR performance and CSR disclosures. Further, some managers fully articulate corporate goals and justify CSR activities in non-strategic terms.

The No Disclosure and No Association hypotheses both share the assumption that real CSR activity is impossible. The difference between these two views is whether or not firms disclose in a neutral or self-serving way. By contrast, both the Positive Association and Full Disclosure hypotheses assume the existence of CSR activities and neutral disclosure. Full Disclosure is simply a more extreme articulation of Positive Association.

PRIOR RESEARCH ON THE ASSOCIATION BETWEEN CORPORATE SOCIAL RESPONSIBILITY DISCLOSURES AND PERFORMANCE

The emphasis in the previous section was on the underlying perspectives and assumptions that generate the alternative views. In this section, we review empirical studies that have assessed both the demand and usefulness of the social responsibility disclosures.

The Demand for Corporate Social Responsibility Disclosures

We first take up the issue of demand. To what extent do regulators require the disclosures of CSR activities? How does the accounting profession view this issue? Finally, to what extent do investors express a desire for CSR disclosures? Unless some investors or other stakeholders demand CSR disclosures, there is little need to pursue the entire issue.

Although, as stated above, most observers characterize social responsibility disclosure as voluntary in nature, the point should not be overstated. For example, Trotman and Bradley (1981) emphasize that since 1973 corporations have been required to disclose "any material impact which compliance with environmental laws would have on capital expenditure, earnings and the company's competitive position" (p. 356).

The 1977 Report of the Advisory Committee on Corporate Disclosure to the Securities and Exchange Commission (SEC) further amplified the agency's position:

The commission requires disclosure of matters of social and environmental significance only when the Commission judges the information in question to be material to informed investment or corporate suffrage decision-making. . . . The Committee also agreed that disclosure should be required when management is engaged in a consistent pattern of violation of law in the social or environmental areas. . . . However, a minority of the Committee disagreed with the position and "believes strongly that disclosure of social and environmental information is material to investment and corporate suffrage decision-making regardless of its economic impact on the financial performance of the company." These members believe that some shareholders are concerned with their company's social performance as such. They also argue that this kind of information reflects on the quality and character of management, which information clearly plays an important role in both investment and corporate suffrage decision-making. The minority would urge the Commission to require increased disclosure in the social and environmental area. (quoted in Trotman and Bradley, 1981)

Thus, the SEC's position, as documented here, requires disclosure of both "social and environmental information" when it will provide investors with knowledge about "financial performance." By contrast, if social and environmental information is not related to purely economic issues, there is no regulatory requirement to disclose this information. Such disclosures are considered discretionary. Thus, the general question about the relationship between CSR performance and financial performance becomes a crucial issue in satisfying SEC requirements. Further, the Advisory Committee's report explicitly acknowledges that some of the members of the committee recognized a demand for social performance information, even in the absence of any direct link with financial performance.

The accounting profession has also addressed the need for increased corporate disclosures of CSR activities. For example, in 1973, the Study Group on the Objectives of Financial Statements proposed that one of the basic objectives of corporate reporting should be "to report on those activities of the enterprise affecting society which can be determined and described or measured and which are important to the role of the enterprise in its environment" (American Institute of Certified Public Accountants, 1973, p. 54). The Study Group's position reflects the more inclusive view suggested by the minority opinion of the previously quoted SEC Advisory Committee. (For additional studies and reports by the accounting profession see American Accounting Association, 1971–1975, 1978; National Association of Accountants, 1974; American Institute of Certified Public Accountants, 1976.)

Undoubtedly, recognition must be given to the dramatic change in disclosure philosophy associated with increasing the set of information called for by advocates of CSR disclosure. Nevertheless, we agree with Spicer's (1978a) conclusion that "there have been mounting social, political and economic pressures on corporate managements to pay greater attention to the wider social and environmental consequences of corporate activities in the decision-making process" (p. 94). These pressures have led to the continued demand for better methods of measuring and reporting CSR activities.

An early piece of evidence suggesting the demand for CSR disclosures even among the most sophisticated investors was provided by Longstreth and Rosenbloom (1973). The authors reported survey results for 196 institutional investors. About 60 percent of the respondents agreed that when making investment decisions, in addition to examining traditional financial criteria, they also considered social factors. Further, about half of the respondents who looked at social criteria indicated that they did so to avoid certain investments that they perceived as being socially undesirable, immoral, or contrary to institutional purposes.

Similarly, Buzby and Falk (1978), based on their survey of the information needs of mutual fund managers, concluded that pollution performance disclosure was ranked as important information.

More recently, Dierkes and Antal (1985) concluded their review of international surveys on investor needs by noting some interesting general observations. Referring to investor surveys, the authors wrote:

All show that the concept of social reporting, the underlying philosophy of social responsibility, and its public documentations are strongly supported. . . . As regards the second step in determining usefulness, the surveys reveal that although respondents consider the information published to be useful in that it provides more comprehensive knowledge about the companies' activities, there appears to be a general feeling that some of the information is not of priority significance while more important areas are left uncovered. (pp. 31–32)

In other words, while most of the surveys report a strong demand for CSR disclosure, the demand for high quality information is not always being met.

The Empirical Record

Having established the existence of a demand for CSR disclosure among various constituencies, it is useful to turn our attention to the empirical record with regard to the four specific hypotheses discussed above.

Few, if any, researchers have accepted the No Disclosure hypothesis because it simply does not correspond to empirical realities. Even a cursory examination of a random sample of annual reports would indicate the existence of at least some disclosure of CSR activities. Preston (1981), for example, concluded that well over half of the Fortune 500 companies presented some social disclosure material in the annual report. However, he goes on to emphasize that not all companies report the same amount or quality of information. Further, Preston emphasizes that U.S. corporations have tended to emphasize some areas of socially responsible activities over other areas. In his words, "U.S. firms have tended historically to emphasize philanthropic and citizenship roles, and only recently added other areas of external concern to the corporate social agenda. In fact, at the present time basic information about employment structure is rarely made available in the regular public reports of most U.S. companies" (p. 258). Even with these legitimate criticisms, the basic point that some meaningful CSR disclosure exists is not at issue. In addition, Mathews (1993) reviews an impressive list of studies documenting the existence of CSR disclosures.

The No Disclosure hypothesis is too extreme. The Full Disclosure hypothesis has never been formally tested. We, thus, turn our focus to the No Association and Positive Association hypotheses.

The No Association hypothesis has received some empirical support. At least three studies, for example, have concluded that in the area of environmental pollution there is little or no association between disclosures and performance. We briefly summarize these three studies:

Ingram and Frazier (1980)

The authors examined the relationship between environmental disclosure and actual environmental performance. To gauge environmental disclosure, the authors analyzed, on a sentence by sentence basis, the annual reports of 40 companies belonging to one of four highly polluting industries. The study covered the years between 1970 and 1974. The authors correlated the results of the annual report content analysis to an independent evaluation of environmental performance conducted by the CEP.

The authors concluded that the results revealed, at best, only a weak association between quantitative measures of disclosure and social performance. They conjectured that the weak association may be a result of little or no external monitoring of firms' social disclosure. Similar to arguments advanced by Benston, the authors wrote, "Since management is free to use its own discretion in selecting information to be reported, it is possible for poorer performers to bias their selections in order to appear like the better performers" (p. 620).

Freedman and Jaggi (1982)

One of the objectives of this study was to re-examine the degree of association between environmental disclosures and environmental performance. Noting that Ingram and Frazier did not examine 10-K disclosures, but limited their analysis to annual report disclosures, and citing several other weaknesses inherent in their study, the authors re-open the question by applying a different data set and methodology. It should be noted, however, that they continue to rely on the CEP evaluations to measure actual environmental performance.

Even with the methodological improvements, the authors' conclusions, based on the results of an analysis of 31 firms, are in agreement with the previous study. That is, Freedman and Jaggi are unable to reject the null hypothesis of no association between the extensiveness of pollution disclosures and the pollution performance of firms.

Wiseman (1982)

This study represents a third attempt to gauge the degree of association between environmental disclosure and performance. Once again, the author correlates the annual report disclosure of 26 firms versus CEP evaluations, and, once again, the conclusion is that corporate environmental disclosures are "incomplete and are not related to the firms' actual environmental performance" (p. 53).

In contrast to each of these three studies, other researchers have rejected the No Association hypothesis in favor of the Positive Association hypothesis. Evidence in support of a positive association between disclosures and performance, where social responsibility is viewed in more general terms, is provided by the following three studies:

Abbott and Monsen (1979)

"The most basic issue regarding the annual report as a source of social involvement data is whether the reported variation in social activities among firms is a reflection of real activities or is only an index of company policies on communicating activities to shareholders" (p. 506). So begins Abbott and Monsen's empirical study. To further our understanding of CSR disclosure, the authors develop what they term the Social Involvement Disclosure (SID) scale. The scale is created by quantifying annual report disclosures through the application of content analysis. Abbott and Monsen examined annual report disclosures for each of the following areas: environment, equal opportunity, personnel, community involvement, products, and other.

The aggregate SID scores were then compared to independent reputational scales. According to the authors, the correlation between the SID scores and reputational scales was reasonably high. In addition, the authors reported high correlations with two specific issues measured by the SID scale: equal opportunities and community involvement.

Bowman (1984)

Bowman, reflecting the rationale underlying the Positive Association hypothesis, suggested that there are strong reasons to believe that annual reports will reflect the underlying corporate realities. He wrote: "The truth is that the typical chief executive officer spends considerable time outlining the contents of the report, sketching out much of it, and proofreading and changing most of it to his taste. CEOs see annual reports as major communication devices to many constituencies, both internal and external, concerning their and their companies' performances" (p. 63). To test whether annual reports do reflect reality, the author used a list of companies noted as outstanding in their corporate social responsibility activities by Milton Moskowitz, editor of *Business and Society*. The 14 companies were matched by industry and size. Annual report disclosures during 1973 for all companies were coded on a line-by-line basis as to whether or not the line discussed CSR issues.

The reported results clearly support the Positive Association hypothesis. On average, the socially responsible firms were more likely to discuss CSR issues. In fact, for the socially responsible firms, about 5 percent of the disclosures were devoted to this topic. This finding is statistically greater than the 1.74 percent discussion for the control sample. In other words, the companies that were perceived as high in terms of social responsibility reported about three times the average for the randomly chosen matched pair group.

Wolfe (1991)

The most recent study to examine the relationship between CSR disclosure and performance is Wolfe (1991). Using a computer-aided content analysis program, the author developed CSR scores for nine companies. These scores were then compared with *Fortune* magazine's reputational index. The correlation coefficient of .69 was significant at the .05 level.

Although Wolfe believes his positive results are encouraging, the precise relationship between CSR disclosures and CSR performance remains an open question. With important implications for our study, Wolfe concludes that, irrespective of the results of future research to investigate the question of the association between disclosures and performance, he believes that "social reporting, in and of itself, is a corporate behavior worthy of investigation by CSR researchers" (p. 303).

To summarize, based on our review of the available empirical evidence, it is difficult to distinguish between the No Association and Positive Association hypotheses. If pushed, we would conclude that the empirical record marginally favors the Positive Association hypothesis.

Our judgment is tilted toward this hypothesis based on two important qualifications with regard to the existing evidence favoring the No Association hypothesis. First, the evidence in favor of No Association is confined to the single issue of environmental performance. While this issue is important, it tells us little about the general question of CSR disclosures and performance. Second, all three studies used the CEP data to evaluate actual performance. These limitations make it quite difficult to generalize the results.

Although the evidence in favor of Positive Association is less than overwhelming, it is slightly more convincing. For example, each of the three studies reporting positive associations used more general definitions of the CSR phenomenon and did not restrict themselves to a single issue. Second, each of the studies used different reputational indexes to assess actual performance.

Nevertheless, based on our literature review, we express our most important conclusion with no hesitation: there is ample evidence to suggest the importance of reassessing the association between CSR disclosure and actual performance.

NOTES

1.   A similar and perhaps more radical view than Benston's has recently been put forth by Baruch Lev. Accounting researchers are often reticent about offering normative guidelines to corporate managers. Most accounting research is self-described as a branch of "positive" economics. Therefore, it is with great anticipation and interest that one approaches the recent article by Berkeley Professor Baruch Lev where he adopts an unabashedly normative tone (1992).

In this article, Lev suggested that corporate executives involved in financial reporting activities need to evaluate their information disclosure decisions using cost-benefit analysis. He labelled his program "Information Disclosure Strategy." Throughout his analysis, Lev emphasized the need to view disclosure decisions as fundamentally similar to other corporate activities. Accordingly, he began his paper by noting: "Most importantly, disclosure activity does not differ in principle from other corporate activities, such as investment, production, and marketing. Disclosure shares with these activities the fundamental characteristics of providing benefits and incurring costs, and it therefore warrants the careful attention and long-term planning accorded to any major corporate activity. Hence the need for an information disclosure strategy" (p. 10). Copyright © 1992 by The Regents of the University of California. Reprinted from the *California Management Review*, vol. 34, no. 4. By permission of The Regents.

In Chapter 8, we critically examine Lev's analysis and offer an alternative view for disclosure.

2.   Ingram and Frazier (1980) point out that not only are CSR disclosures generally voluntary, but they are usually unaudited. "Few efforts have been made to monitor firms' social activities or to validate their disclosures so that motivation may exist for management to distort voluntary disclosures, to the extent that these disclosures reflect aspects of managements' relative performances" (p. 614).

3.   The Positive Association hypothesis is also consistent with other sets of assumptions. For example, it is possible that false and misleading disclosures about CSR activities might lead to false perceptions about actual CSR performance. Thus, a positive association between CSR disclosure and CSR performance might simply be the result of misinformation and mismeasurement of CSR performance.

5

The Language of Corporate Social Responsibility: Methodology and Results

The goal of the second phase of the study is to determine whether or not socially responsible firms signal their identity through the annual report. To this end, the single most important issue is the selection of empirical proxies to measure the two key variables: corporate social responsibility (CSR) performance and CSR disclosures. Our estimates of CSR performance are based on an analysis completed by the Council on Economic Priorities (CEP) (1991). To develop a proxy for CSR disclosures, we utilized a methodology known as content analysis. This methodology has been advocated both in the CSR literature and beyond.[1]

CORPORATE SOCIAL RESPONSIBILITY PERFORMANCE

In particular, we examine CSR disclosures for a group of 33 firms that have been identified by the CEP as being socially responsible (Group 1) and compare their 1989 disclosures to a control sample matched by both industry and size (Group 2). Ingram (1978); Trotman and Bradley (1981); Cowen, Ferreri, and Parker (1987); and Roberts (1992) suggest the importance of both industry and size as factors affecting CSR disclosures. The sample size was reduced because the presidents' letters were not available for all firms examined in Part I. Appendix B.2 provides the names of the 66 companies included for analysis.

Drawing on the holdings listed in the prospectuses of the socially responsible mutual funds, and based on their own analyses, the CEP described the companies in Group 1 as "ethical" portfolio companies. The advantages of choosing the CEP firms for our study have been discussed in Chapter 3. The CEP is one of the most highly regarded external producers of social responsibility information.

CORPORATE SOCIAL
RESPONSIBILITY DISCLOSURES

Content analysis is a relatively new methodology that has proved useful in analyzing written texts. Bowman (1984), in emphasizing the use and importance of the methodology, suggested that content analysis provided a "gestalt, not readily available through other methods" (p. 62). The method consists of codifying qualitative information in literary form into meaningful categories, where categories are defined as precisely as possible with regard to the hypotheses being tested. The results of the analysis can then be transformed into quantitative scales, allowing for comparison among different literary documents (Abbott and Monsen, 1979; Ingram and Frazier, 1980) .

The most important methodological steps involved in content analysis are the following: determine the sampling unit, determine the recording units, and determine the themes and categories to be used in the coding (Wolfe, 1991).

The sampling unit chosen for this study was the president's letter to shareholders (step 1). Each paragraph of the letter was viewed as a recording unit (step 2). Our choice of paragraphs rather than sentences or words was influenced both by our research objectives and by a test code of sample texts that indicated that using paragraphs would enhance reliability.

Within the president's letter we identified paragraphs as belonging to one of two major classificatory themes: general corporate goals or specific CSR activities (step 3).

General Corporate Goals

Paragraphs were identified in which a general articulation of corporate goals was provided. Specifically, we categorized each of these paragraphs as follows:

The paragraph suggests that among the most important goals of this corporation are:
maximizing shareholder value;

increasing shareholder value;

achieving well-defined financial targets (for example, return on equity, return on sales, market share, earnings per share, or market return);

producing highest quality products or services for customers; or

satisfying the demands of important stakeholders. Stakeholders could include shareholders and customers, but must also include at least one of the following: creditors, employees, suppliers, government, community, or society at large.

An example of each should help clarify:

Maximizing Shareholder Value

These objectives and strategies remain part of the corporation's culture, committing us to maximizing value for our shareholders — as a successful, independent marketer of leading consumer brands — by balancing competitive current returns with investment in profitable growth for the future.

Increasing Shareholder Value

We pledge to continue increasing both the value of your company and the dependable flow of dividend payments that has now risen each year for 15 consecutive years.

Achieving Well-defined Financial Targets

The focus of the entire organization is on achieving target profitability. And this year should be much improved. . . . We continue to target 5 percent return on sales as the chief measure of our success.

Producing Highest Quality Products

We believe much of this growth is a reflection of our commitment to 100 percent customer satisfaction. We can now say with confidence that the progress we have made during the past year has firmly established our company as one of the few viable participants in the air express industry.

Satisfying the Demands of Important Stakeholders

Throughout this year and beyond, we hope to "refine the bottom line" and look for more and more ways of running an innovative business for the benefit of our stockholders, our customers, our employees, and our community.

Corporate Social Responsibility Activities

In addition to classifying corporate goals, paragraphs were identified in which the author explicitly indicated that the company was engaged in one or more of the following socially responsible activities:

donates corporate funds to charitable causes;

is actively engaged in meeting environmental concerns;

has an employee stock ownership program;

links employee performance with rewards (salary, benefits, promotion, etc.);

promotes increased employee autonomy and responsibility;

seeks out women and minorities for hiring or promotion;

is helping to solve national social problems in addition to environmental concerns (crime, unemployment, education, health care, etc.);

is meeting local community needs (unemployment, education, day care, museums, etc.);

avoids nuclear energy;

avoids military contracts; and

is involved in other socially responsible activities.

Once a paragraph was identified as articulating a specific CSR activity, independent raters were asked to determine whether or not a formal justification for the activity was provided. (Raters did not know the identity of the companies because references to company names were eliminated.)

Raters were asked to consider carefully the context of the statement and indicate whether or not justification for the activity (or avoidance of activity) is explicitly provided. If the author provided justification, raters were asked if the justification was of a strategic or non-strategic nature, or both. Following Goodpaster, a strategic justification explicitly links the activity to enhanced corporate financial performance and views the activity instrumentally, as a means toward achieving a financial objective. Examples include increasing profits, boosting sales, raising margins, enhancing operating efficiency, or expanding operating flexibility. A non-strategic justification would be a formal statement explaining a given activity that did not link it to financial performance. Key words or phrases include social responsibility, community responsibility, obligations, ethics, morality, or fairness. This methodology resulted in a 91 percent inter-rater reliability.

Examples of both strategic and non-strategic justifications should help clarify. One of the companies in our sample justified its employee stock ownership program as follows: "We anticipate the ESOP [Employee Stock Option Program] will enhance stockholder values by more closely aligning the interests of our personnel and company stockholders, and by providing us with a cost-efficient mechanism to make matching contributions under the savings plan." This company explicitly linked the employee stock ownership program to financial performance. The statement is clear and direct. By implementing this new compensation practice the firm expects to enhance stockholder values. Therefore, this statement is characterized as strategic.

Additional examples of strategic justifications follow:

Increasing Employee Autonomy: The development of an entrepreneurial spirit within the Company will provide the flexibility to assure profitability growth in the years ahead.

Seeks Out Women and Minorities: The Hudson Institute has predicted that 85 percent of all entry level jobs between now and the year 2000 will be filled by women, minorities, and immigrants. Those companies that become attractive places for these people to work will be the companies that succeed in the 1990s.

Engaged in Meeting Environmental Concerns: While we saw significant potential for parts cleaner services in the industrial market, we also saw opportunities to help industrial plants with other hazardous waste disposal problems. Tens of thousands of industrial plants use solvents, paint thinners, lubricating oils, coolants, and a variety of other fluids. Many of these fluids are considered to be hazardous and must be disposed of in accordance with Federal and State Environmental Regulation. Companies that generate small quantities of these fluids find coping with the environmental regulations and proper disposal to be particularly cumbersome, because they might not have in-house expertise in all of the various environmental regulations.

The language used to justify these activities contrasts with the non-strategic language employed in the following examples:

Donates Corporate Funds to Charitable Causes: Last year, we celebrated the ten year anniversary of the opening of our doors in the old gas station in Burlington. In looking back over what we have accomplished in our first ten years, we probably take most pride in our growing reputation as one of the most socially responsible businesses in America. The Council on Economic Priorities recently honored our Company with the "Corporate Conscience Award for Corporate Giving." The award was given in recognition of our Company's policy of donating 7.5 percent of our pretax

income to social service agencies and community causes through the
corporate foundation.

Is Helping to Solve National Social Problems: Our efforts to relocate manufacturing and increasingly, R&D internationally are designed to make an
ongoing contribution to every society in which we operate. . . . It also
demonstrates the corporation's desire to help move international trade
toward greater equilibrium.

Seeks Out Women and/or Minorities: As we move ahead, we renew our commitment to equal opportunity and diversity throughout the corporation as
expressed on the cover of this report. That commitment runs top to bottom.
We believe in it.

Links Employee Performance With Rewards: The Company recognizes that
many employees invest significant portions of their lives in their jobs and
that they make many significant contributions to its growth and success.
Believing that it is in the best interests of all employees, the Company has
adopted a "Security of Employment Plan" for the purpose of providing
some financial stability to employees whose employment is terminated
following a change of control in the Company.

These examples illustrate the distinction between strategic and non-
strategic justifications. In the first example, the company explicitly uses
the term "social responsibility." The second example justifies its
increased international activities by stating that it fulfills the corporate
"desire to move international trade toward greater equilibrium." The
third example defends the company's stance of equal employment opportunities and diversity in the workplace by simply noting, "We believe in
it." Finally, notice in the last example that the letter to shareholders
simply takes it as self-evident that because employees invest significant
portions of their lives working for the corporation, the corporation has an
obligation to do what is in the "best interest of all employees." In each of
the cases, the corporation justifies a particular activity not because it will
enhance corporate profits but for non-strategic reasons. The authors of
these letters assume the reader will understand and accept corporate
responsibilities beyond financial and legal concerns.

RESULTS: DO SOCIALLY RESPONSIBLE
FIRMS SIGNAL THEIR IDENTITIES?

The annual report to shareholders, and specifically the president's
letter, provides a potential medium for management to voluntarily signal
and justify CSR activities. Specifically, we ask and answer each of the
following questions:

Are companies that have been perceived as meeting CSR criteria more likely than non-socially responsible companies to communicate CSR activities? Specifically, which types of activities do the two groups disclose?

Do companies that have been perceived as meeting CSR criteria communicate corporate goals in ways that can be distinguished from non-socially responsible firms?

Are companies justifying CSR activities using language that can be described as non-strategic?

The answers to these three questions will allow us to distinguish among the No Association, Positive Association, and Full Disclosure hypotheses.

Our results show that companies identified as meeting CSR criteria (Group 1) are more than twice as likely to disclose activities related to CSR than the control sample (Group 2). Group 1 firms reported 56 activities versus 25 for the Group 2 firms. This difference is statistically significant using the appropriate t-test. In addition, we examine the data using a non-parametric sign-test. Again, the differences between the two samples are significant at the .01 level. These results are shown in Table 5.1.

A positive association characterizes the relationship between CSR disclosures (through the president's letter to shareholders) and CSR performance. This conclusion is neither driven by a small number of Group 1 firms reporting many CSR activities nor is it driven by Group 1 firms focusing only on a small number of CSR activities. In fact, a careful examination of the results indicates the opposite is true. Comparing the 33 matched pairs shows that in 20 cases the Group 1 firms have more disclosures than the Group 2 firms. In only six cases did the Group 2 firms have more disclosures than the Group 1 firms. In seven cases, groups 1 and 2 reported the same number of CSR activities. Further, the single activity — out of 11 potential activities — in which the Group 2 firms have more disclosures than the Group 1 counterparts was "links employee performance with reward," arguably the least relevant category in terms of pure CSR.

Examining specific types of disclosures reveals that the most important differences between the two groups are in the following three areas:

Is helping to solve national social problems in addition to environmental concerns (Group 1: 14 disclosures, Group 2: 4 disclosures, significant at .01 level);

TABLE 5.1
Corporate Social Responsibility Activities and Their Justifications

CSR Activity	Group 1, CSR Firms					Group 2, Control Firms				
	N.J.	S.J.	N-S.J.	Both	Totals	N.J.	S.J.	N-S.J.	Both	Totals
Donates corporate funds to charitable causes	1	0	2	0	3	0	0	1	0	1
Is actively engaged in meeting environmental concerns	0	3	0	1	4**	0	0	0	0	0
Has an employee stock ownership program	0	3	0	3	6	0	2	1	0	3
Links employee performance with rewards (salary, benefits, promotion, etc.)	1	1	1	1	4	0	1	1	4	6
Promotes increased employee autonomy and responsibility	4	9	0	1	14	1	7	0	0	8
Seeks out women and/or minorities for hiring and/or promotion	0	3	1	0	4	0	0	1	0	1
Is helping to solve national social problems in addition to environmental concerns (crime, unemployment, education, health care, etc.)	2	3	5	4	14***	1	0	2	1	4
Is meeting local community needs (unemployment, education, museums, etc.)	1	0	2	2	5*	0	1	0	0	1
Avoids nuclear energy	0	0	0	0	0	0	0	0	0	0
Avoids military contracts	0	0	0	0	0	0	0	0	0	0
Other socially responsible activities	1	2	0	0	3	0	0	0	1	1
TOTALS	10	24	11	12	57***	2	11	6	6	25

Notes:
N.J. = No justification for activity provided. S.J. = Strategic justification for activity provided. N-S.J. = Non-strategic justification for activity provided. Both = Both strategic and non-strategic justifications for activity provided. **Group 1 result is significantly higher than Group 2 result at the .05 level. ***Group 1 result is significantly higher than Group 2 result at the .01 level. *Group 1 result is signficantly higher than Group 2 result at the .10 level.

Is actively engaged in meeting environmental concerns (Group 1: 4 disclosures, Group 2: 0 disclosures, significant at .05 level); and

Is meeting local community needs (Group 1: 5 disclosures, Group 2: 1 disclosure, significant at .10 level).

In addition to these statistically significant results, the Group 1 firms were more likely to report information about

charitable donations (Group 1: 3 disclosures, Group 2: 1 disclosure);

the existence of employee stock ownership programs (Group 1: 6 disclosures, Group 2: 3 disclosures);

promotion of increased employee autonomy (Group 1: 14 disclosures, Group 2: 8 disclosures); and

seeking out women and minorities for hiring and promotion (Group 1: 4 disclosures, Group 2: 1 disclosure).

Thus, the evidence unambiguously confirms that managers of CSR firms, consistent with the Positive Association hypothesis, are much more likely to report about CSR activities than the control sample.

Table 5.2 allows us to draw an even stronger conclusion. Examination of our tabulation of articulated corporate goals indicates an important and consistent distinction between the two groups of firms. One of the most important findings of this study is that more than half of the Group

TABLE 5.2
Corporate Goals

Articulated Corporate Goal	Group 1 Totals	Group 2 Totals
Maximizing shareholder value	3	1
Increasing shareholder value	26	23
Achieving well-defined financial targets (for example, return on equity, return on sales, market share, earnings per share, or market return)	8*	3
Producing highest quality products or services for customers	17	14
Satisfying the demands of important stakeholders; stakeholders could include shareholders and customers, but must also include at least one of the following: creditors, employees, suppliers, government, community, or society at large	17***	5

*Group 1 result is signficantly higher than Group 2 result at the .10 level.
***Group 1 result is signficantly higher than Group 2 result at the .01 level.

1 firms (17 of 33) articulated that an important goal of the corporation was "Satisfying the demands of important stakeholders." Stakeholders could include shareholders and customers, but must also include at least one of the following: creditors, employees, suppliers, government, community, or society at large. By contrast, only five of the Group 2 firms explicitly articulated this objective. This difference is significant at the .01 level. The result corroborates the results reported in Table 5.1 and lends strong credence to the Positive Association hypothesis as opposed to the No Association hypothesis.

In addition to the statistically significant results, the Group 1 firms are also more likely to describe "well-defined financial targets (for example, return on equity, return on sales, market share, earnings per share, or market return)" as an important objective (Group 1: 8, Group 2: 3, significant at .10 level). This result, in line with the results above, suggests more precise objectives on the part of the CSR firms than the control sample.

Interestingly, only 4 firms out of the entire sample of 66 explicitly indicated "maximizing shareholder value" as a corporate objective, whereas 49 firms out of the entire sample explicitly indicated "increasing shareholder value" as an objective. Regardless of whether a firm was identified as having met CSR criteria or not, managers are apparently extremely reluctant to invoke the language of maximization. If one takes these results at face value, they conflict sharply with the traditional economic assumption of managerial behavior. Even if one suggests that there need be no link between statements located in the president's letter to shareholders and actual managerial actions, the findings suggest an interesting puzzle; if managers are really attempting to maximize profits, why do they not admit it to shareholders?

The results discussed thus far lead us to conclude in favor of the Positive Association hypothesis. Further, the results about corporate goals provide some preliminary support for the Full Disclosure hypothesis. The Full Disclosure hypothesis, while assuming a positive association between CSR disclosures and performance, also predicts, in part, that managers fully articulate corporate goals. Our result, which shows CSR firms are much more likely to articulate satisfying stakeholder demands (in addition to shareholders and customers) as a corporate goal, provides some evidence in favor of this hypothesis.

We now turn to a discussion of how firms justify CSR activities. This additional evidence again lends support to the Positive Association hypothesis as opposed to the No Association hypothesis. It also provides additional support for the Full Disclosure hypothesis. We note the following four observations:

1. Of the 81 CSR activities disclosed (groups 1 and 2 combined), 21 percent (17 out of 81) were justified using non-strategic language. Further, removing the effects of the 12 activities for which no justification was offered, the data show that 25 percent (17 out of 69), or one out of four disclosures, were justified using purely non-strategic rationales. These data do not necessarily suggest that 25 percent of the activities were originally conceived and undertaken for non-strategic reasons. Many of the activities may well have been selected to increase financial returns, that is, for strategic reasons. Rather, what the data do tell us is that, after the fact, the president's letter to shareholders justifies the socially responsible activities using a significant amount of non-strategic language.

2. Managers will use non-strategic language to justify corporate activities. This finding is strengthened if we include those activities in which the letter used both strategic and non-strategic language to justify the same activity. Twenty-one percent (17 out of 81) of the total CSR activities were justified using a combination of reasons. Therefore, by combining non-strategic justifications with justifications using both strategic and non-strategic language we find that 42 percent of all CSR activities were justified using some non-strategic language. We can push further and state that, of the 69 activities in which some justification was provided, just under half used at least some non-strategic justification (as opposed to pure strategic justification).

3. Of the 81 CSR activities disclosed, the most likely set of activities that was justified using either pure non-strategic language or both non-strategic and strategic languages combined was those activities designed to help solve national social problems. Forty-one percent (7 out of 17) of the pure non-strategic justifications were associated with this category.

4. Comparing the results of groups 1 and 2 shows that Group 1 firms were almost twice as likely to justify activities using non-strategic language (Group 1: 11 non-strategic justifications, Group 2: 6 non-strategic justifications). Similarly, the Group 1 firms were almost twice as likely to justify activities using both strategic and non-strategic justifications (Group 1: 11 combination justifications, Group 2: 6 combination justifications). These results should not be overstated. While it is certain that Group 1 firms are more likely to use some non-strategic justification, this may simply be due to the finding that they are much more likely to disclose CSR activities. (For example, if we look at non-strategic

justifications as a percentage of all CSR activities, the Group 2 firms are actually more likely to use non-strategic language.)

The above evidence supporting the existence of non-strategic justifications for CSR activities can be interpreted in at least two distinct ways. First, it may simply indicate a sensitivity and a response to outside pressure groups. If we maintain, as Benston would have it, that shareholders, managers, and customers are opposed to CSR and view it, at best, as a drain on corporate resources, these non-strategic justifications are merely, to quote Benston, "self-serving exercises" (p. 100). The non-strategic language is used to bluff pressure groups. According to this interpretation, the non-strategic justifications are meaningless ornaments and are understood as such by managers and shareholders in the know. Hence, the non-strategic justifications really constitute a different level of strategic justification.

Strategically speaking, it is in the interest of the corporation to use non-strategic language. Undoubtedly, this view probably can explain some of the non-strategic justifications. The following example of employee-related activity would seem to support such an interpretation.

In the fourth quarter, we established a provision of $78 million after tax to cover closing of the Chicago plant and certain operating departments at other U.S. plants in connection with the consolidation of their production at other manufacturing locations. The provision will cover the write-off of assets as well as retraining, relocation, separation allowances, and other personnel-related costs where applicable. Our paramount concern will be to ease the dislocation burden to our employees and to assist them during the transition period.

Nevertheless, we believe that it is not a full explanation; the strategic use of non-strategic language would seem to be a poor strategy. Why would pressure groups be expected to accept the bluff? Noting that the position assumes that managers and shareholders are not fooled, would pressure groups not possess equal sophistication? Over time, at least, the strategy would become self-defeating.

By contrast, the examples of non-strategic justification in the president's letter to shareholders is also consistent with the view articulated above; real CSR activity exists. This constitutes a second interpretation of the results. Non-strategic justifications exist because managers believe that some non-strategic justifications represent legitimate corporate concerns. While clearly an alternative to the classical view of the corporation, this explanation avoids the major limitation noted above.

Based on the four observations outlined above and regardless of how one interprets the data, the empirical results provide strong evidence in favor of accepting the Positive Association hypothesis and rejecting the No Association hypothesis. The results also strongly support the Full Disclosure hypothesis. Managers justify at least some CSR activities using non-strategic language. Further, Group 1 firms are more likely than Group 2 firms to invoke non-strategic language.

CONCLUSION

We began this phase of the study with a question: Do socially responsible firms signal their identities through the annual report? Our evidence suggests that the answer to this question is yes. There exists a positive association between CSR performance (based on CEP analysis) and CSR disclosures (based on content analysis of the president's letter to shareholders). We do not find these results surprising. Executives of major corporations perceive CSR activities as legitimate endeavors. Therefore, they conclude both that it is in their own interests and that they have obligations to carefully craft and prepare the president's letter to shareholders in order to effectively communicate corporate responsibilities and activities undertaken to satisfy them.

NOTE

1.   For interesting examples of the use of content analysis outside the area of CSR, see Ingram and Frazier (1983); Staw, McKenzie, and Puffer (1983); and Bowman (1984).

III

THE LEGITIMACY OF CORPORATE SOCIAL RESPONSIBILITY

To what extent should the position draw on individual rights, to what degree should it be based on obligations to the community? Wherein lies the proper balance? While no simple guideline suggests itself, the social-historical context provides an important criterion: societies that lean heavily in one direction tend to "correct" in the other.

— Etzioni, 1991, p. 67

6

Criteria for Evaluating the Legitimacy of Corporate Social Responsibility Projects

In parts I and II of this book, the issue of legitimacy was taken for granted. While this working assumption was useful for generating our empirical results, in this chapter, and in chapters 7 and 8, the issue of legitimacy is explored more fully. Given that social responsibility projects entail costs, it is not always obvious under what precise conditions managers will have a responsibility to engage in activities primarily designed to promote societal goals. Thus, in this chapter we discuss four distinct criteria for evaluating the legitimacy of corporate projects for institutionalizing social responsibility: local knowledge, level of responsibility, shared consensus, and relationship to financial performance. We conclude our discussion by noting that in those cases where the firm possesses knowledge about a specific problem and its solution, is directly responsible for causing harm, where a shared consensus among all relevant stakeholders exists, and financial performance will be enhanced social responsibility projects are ideal.

In Chapter 7, we examine five specific proposals for promoting corporate social responsibility (CSR) goals. The issues to be dealt with are corporate charity, corporate codes of conduct, employee autonomy, worksite health promotion, and changing the structure of corporate boards. Each of these five proposals deals with changing internal corporate procedures rather than those proposals designed to impose changes from the outside (government regulation, consumer boycotts, etc.). These proposals, therefore, provide useful and illuminating examples to illustrate the model developed in this chapter. Finally, in Chapter 8 we extend our discussion by examining the issue of financial disclosure.

One of the main goals of Part III is to discover the ways in which CSR practitioners craft programs to find the appropriate balance among the four criteria developed here. No program will meet all of the criteria. In fact, our model specifically suggests that there is often a trade-off between the first three criteria and the last. For example, in those situations where the corporation directly imposes harm on third parties and where a high degree of consensus exists among all stakeholders (see especially our discussion of financial disclosure in Chapter 8), there is little need to link the social responsibility program to financial performance. By contrast, as the corporation seeks proactive solutions to problems that are only incidental to the corporation and where little consensus exists, the predicted relationship to financial performance becomes more crucial. By formally examining the trade-offs among these four criteria we more fully understand the complex relationship between social responsibility and financial impacts.

LOCAL KNOWLEDGE

To design effective programs to satisfy social responsibilities, the organization must possess knowledge about the specific social problem. For example, before a company can be expected to institutionalize a factory safety program, managers must be aware of the dangers inherent in their production processes. If decision makers within the corporation are ignorant about a particular problem, it will be impossible for them to develop reasonable solutions.

Further, decision makers must possess knowledge about the organizations' own abilities to deal with a specific situation. Only decision makers intimately familiar with organizational capabilities can appropriately assess a given situation. By matching their own expertise to specific social problems, corporations can potentially meet perceived social obligations.

Local knowledge is generated in many ways. The success or failure of social responsibility projects is often a function of the manner in which the knowledge is obtained. One way for a company to learn more about its responsibilities is through the activities of pressure groups and other interested parties. Groups external to the corporation may seek to educate the company about particular social responsibilities. In this way, knowledge about particular problems may be thrust upon a reluctant management. The details of recently settled federal class action suits against Denny's restaurant chain, a Fortune 500 company, illustrate the limitations of relying solely on outsiders. In settling the cases, Denny's agreed to pay $54 million.

According to the New York *Times* report (May 29, 1994), more than 4,300 complaints were lodged against the company for discriminating against minority customers. The U.S. Justice Department claimed that the incidents of bias against thousands of black customers involved refused service or being forced to wait longer or pay more than white customers. Jerome J. Richardson, the chief executive of Denny's parent company, Flagstar Companies, insists that complaints about service are inevitable in a gigantic chain like Denny's. While Richardson may be correct that complaints are inevitable, it might also be suggested that systematic complaints of bias deserve the scrutiny of top management. Had Denny's created and acted on its own information about alleged policies of discrimination, rather than merely reacting to legal claims, the company might well have limited its exposure.

Often, local knowledge about social responsibilities exists as a by-product of other routine operating events or activities. Local knowledge about social responsibilities is discovered in indirect ways. A new employee, for example, may uncover information about a history of fraudulent financial reporting. Such was the case with Prudential and Mark Jorgensen.

After managing the real estate portfolio for the California State Teachers Retirement System, in May 1992 Mark Jorgensen joined Prudential to manage part of the prestigious Prudential Property Investment Separate Account. Jorgensen replaced Charles Lightner, who had recently been promoted. After touring numerous real estate holdings, Jorgensen claimed to have discovered that the appraisal values of some of the properties were highly inflated. One effect of the overvaluation was to mislead investors and potential investors about the real worth of the portfolio. In addition, the company's fees for managing the funds were inflated as a result of the overvaluation.

Initially, Jorgensen thought that the outside appraisers were to blame. But, according to Jorgensen, when confronted, Lightner admitted he was responsible. Jorgensen decided to bring the information to the attention of the legal department. According to a New York *Times* article (May 25, 1994), a company lawyer, Ray Giordano, interviewed Jorgensen.

About a month later, Jorgensen received a memo stating that he was to take a paid leave of absence. The company was apparently aggressively pursuing accusations of wrongdoing against Jorgensen, claiming that he had mislead clients about overvaluations. After deciding to sue

Prudential, Jorgensen was fired for unethical conduct in filing the confidential records.

Fortunately for Jorgensen, the story did not end here. In response to intense and continued pressure from concerned customers, Prudential launched a second investigation conducted by outside lawyers and accountants. On April 28, 1994, Jorgensen met with chief executive officer (CEO) Robert Winters. Winters apologized to Jorgensen and told him that the company recognized that he had been correct. Investors were being fully informed and compensated. Lightner was asked to resign.

In this case, Prudential accidentally discovered a breach of a fiduciary responsibility to investors. The new employee vigorously pursued the issue. How companies respond to this kind of information is a crucial component to CSR. Even in the best companies, creating an environment conducive to truth-telling is not a trivial task. As in this case, powerful institutional or personal barriers may exist.

Many firms will, therefore, actively seek out local knowledge about social problems and their solutions. In fact, promoting the creation of this type of knowledge may itself be a component of CSR.

According to Donna J. Wood (1994), "boundary spanners" can be helpful in uncovering new and emerging issues and gathering information. Wood writes, "Boundary spanners are the people who gather information from and conduct transactions with stakeholders in the environment. Like the double-faced Roman god Janus, boundary spanners look both ways — inside and out — serving as gatekeepers for information and interpretations" (p. 196).

Only through an active stance toward the creation of social responsibility knowledge can a firm hope to completely fulfill its mandate. As Wood further notes, by self-consciously changing the organization, top management can respond appropriately to changes in the external environment. Wood suggests the following formal organizational changes:

professionalize the boundary spanning role and give it higher status;

when needed, create specialized units for key boundary spanning functions;

provide enough autonomy to boundary spanners;

make sure boundary agents have ready access to top decision makers; and

listen to and act on the information and suggestions of boundary spanners. (pp. 200–201)

These prescriptions seem particularly well-suited for the two cases discussed above. Denny's had ample opportunity to create a specialized unit to investigate the more than 4,300 complaints. Had this unit been given autonomy and access to top decision makers, management naturally would have listened to and acted on the information. The existence of a specialized unit would have made it virtually impossible for the organization to continue ignoring the complaints. Similarly, the Prudential case might have been resolved at a much earlier and less public stage if Jorgensen had access to top decision makers. In fact, Jorgensen himself stated his desire to meet with Winters at a July 30 meeting with a Prudential lawyer. According to the New York *Times* report, the lawyer scoffed. "Did Mr. Jorgensen think the head of such a huge company would throw open his doors, thank him for his honesty and, on Mr. Jorgensen's word, dismiss Mr. Lightner?" The irony here is that the head of the huge company did eventually throw open his doors, although on terms much less advantageous to the organization than might have been.

Understanding the process of how local knowledge about social responsibilities is created and exploited within the organization is a fundamental key to evaluating social responsibility programs. Local knowledge is such a crucial variable in evaluating CSR that David L. Engel (1979) has argued that, at least in some cases, the mere existence of private local knowledge constitutes the single strongest defense for corporate altruism.

Engel's argument is based on the intuitive appeal of the following proposition: "If I find myself specially well situated to improve A's lot, at cost to myself that I am reasonably certain will be vastly less than the gain to A, I should do so" (p. 60). This proposition has been labelled the Kew Gardens Principle. Its most dramatic instantiation is the story of Kitty Genovese, who was brutally murdered in the Kew Gardens section of Queens, New York. The public outrage at the lack of any response or help from the numerous witnesses to the crime underscores the general acceptance of the proposition.

Engel believes that situations in which a corporation possesses local knowledge about harm it may inflict on society (for example, the environmental dangers of a particular production process), and where the legislature is ignorant about the dangers inherent in the new process, provide the most defensible case for altruistic behavior on the part of the corporation. In Engel's words:

In short, in order for the suggested Kew Gardens principle to justify corporate altruism other than disclosure (at least in the first instance), the argument must be (a) that the substantive problem is a new one, and (b) that the Kew Gardens principle will be offended by profit-maximizing corporate conduct before the legislature will have a chance to act. Such a temporary social emergency might arise, for example, in a pollution emergency of unanticipated severity, in which the pollution tax levels set by the legislature or agency were not adequate to shut down a plant completely but in which continued operation would plainly offend the Kew Gardens principle. The desire to maintain good will might allow the profit motive itself to take care of such a case. But if it did not, substantive corporate voluntarism would seem appropriate. (p. 68-69)

The key issue in legitimizing CSR, according to Engel, is possession of private local knowledge. We close this section by noting that, while we concur with Engel about the centrality of this variable, it is by no means the only available criterion to evaluate CSR activities.

LEVEL OF RESPONSIBILITY

One of the most important distinctions that managers must make to determine the legitimacy of social responsibility programs is whether or not the corporation is responsible for a particular situation. If managers and other stakeholders determine a cause and effect link between corporate activities and the suffering of a particular group, we suggest that it is almost universally accepted that corporations are expected to seek solutions. In this case, corporations must either cease from engaging in the harmful activities, compensate victims, or both.

The controversial actions and statements of the tobacco industry over the past four decades are illustrative here. The tobacco industry represents a huge and politically sensitive sector of the U.S. economy. During 1993, the five largest domestic producers (RJR Nabisco Holdings, American Brands, Universal, Standard Commercial, UST, and Dibrell Brothers) generated nearly $30 billion in sales and $815 million in profits. The industry's return on stockholders' equity of 16.5 percent was second only to the pharmaceutical industry. The industry directly employed 4,600 people. The importance of the industry, however, reaches beyond U.S. borders. In fact, financial analysts believe the key to sustained success in the industry is the projected robust volume growth outside the U.S. Some analysts predict export volume to grow by more than 10 percent per year for the remainder of the decade.

The profound and excruciatingly difficult practical and moral problem for the industry can be outlined as follows:

Premise A: Tobacco companies manufacture huge numbers of cigarettes.

Premise B: There is near consensus in the scientific community that cigarette smoking is harmful to health.

Conclusion: Therefore, there exists a direct cause and effect link between corporate activities of tobacco companies and the suffering of a particular group, namely smokers.

The implications of the above syllogism are clear-cut. The core activity of tobacco companies violates one of the most basic notions of CSR. No doubt, the executives of tobacco companies, currently under intense public scrutiny, are well aware of this difficult situation. In the words of one high level executive,

It was very difficult when you were asked, as chairman of a tobacco company, to discuss the health question on television. You had not only your own business to consider but the employees throughout the industry, retailers, consumers, farmers growing the leaf, and so on, and you were in a much too responsible position to get up and say: "I accept that the product which we and all our competitors are putting on the market gives you lung cancer; whatever you might think privately." (Anthony D. McCormick, former chairman of Batco, as quoted by the New York *Times*, June 16, 1994)

Whether or not one accepts the assertion that executives could be "too responsible" to articulate private beliefs, the quote shows the stakes are high; peoples' lives and livelihoods are at risk.

The tobacco industry's response to the increasing evidence of the toxic nature of cigarettes has evolved over time. The overarching strategy, however, has been to attack each of the elements in the syllogism described above. Unfortunately for the industry, this three-pronged attack has proved self-defeating.

To combat Premise A, tobacco companies would not stop manufacturing huge numbers of cigarettes, but rather would begin researching the possibility of manufacturing a new kind of cigarette. The new cigarette would give the consumer the pleasure of a traditional cigarette, but would be a much safer product.

Brown and Williamson Tobacco Corporation, for example, engaged in a major research project beginning in the 1960s. According to internal documents obtained by the New York *Times* (June 17, 1994), the company investigated the possibility of producing a cigarette that would significantly cut down on tobacco contents. The proposed device relied on heating rather than burning. In spite of the early optimism reflected in the comments of researchers, Project Ariel, as it was called, proved unsuccessful. In fact, by 1983 all three of the leading cigarette companies closed their research laboratories. One reason the companies ceased research activities was probably the belief that it would be difficult to market the new, safer cigarettes. The cigarette produced by Brown and Williamson, for example, gave smokers an uncomfortable jolt. A second reason for closing the laboratories, however, had nothing to do with consumer preferences, but rather was based on the fear of possible legal complications. The internal research studies were corroborating the negative findings of a direct link between cigarette smoking and health hazards. The Brown and Williamson documents indicate that lawyers may have advised corporate executives to remove the files containing some of these research findings.

The inherent weakness of the industry's attempt to produce a safer cigarette was neatly summarized by William W. Reid, a researcher from Batco's Australian affiliate. "No industry was going to accept that its product was toxic, or even believe it to be so, and naturally when the health question was first raised we had to start by denying it at the P.R. [public relations] level. By continuing that policy we had got ourselves into a corner and left no room to maneuver. In other words, if we did get a breakthrough and were able to improve our product, we should have to about-face, and this was practically impossible at the P.R. level" (New York *Times*, June 16, 1994).

Partially as a result of the failure to successfully develop and market a safer cigarette, the industry shifted its strategy for dealing with the problem. Rather than altering the product, industry spokesmen began to deny vigorously the validity of Premise B more than ever. Edward Horrigan, Jr., the chairman and chief executive of the Ligget Group, testified in 1982 before Congress as follows: "After three decades of investigation and millions of dollars invested by the government, the tobacco industry and private organizations, the smoking and health controversy remains unresolved. The net result of all this effort has been no causal link between smoking and disease has been established. This is not merely the opinion of tobacco industry executives. This is scientific fact readily available to anyone willing to make an objective, unemotional study of the existing evidence." This view, a direct assault on Premise B, is not unique. More recently, Andrew W. Tisch, the chairman and chief executive of the Lorillard Tobacco Company, testified similarly on April 14, 1994, before U.S. Representative Henry Waxman's Congressional Subcommittee on Tobacco. The exchange went as follows:

Mr. Waxman: In a deposition last year you were asked whether cigarette smoking causes cancer. Your answer was, "I don't believe so." Do you stand by that answer today?

Mr. Tisch: I do, sir.

Mr. Waxman: Do you understand how isolated you are in the belief from the entire scientific community?

Mr. Tisch: I do, sir.

Mr. Waxman: You're the head of a manufacturer of a product that's been accused by the overwhelming scientific community to cause cancer. You don't know? Do you have an interest in finding out?

Mr. Tisch: I do, sir, yes.

Mr. Waxman: And what have you done to pursue that interest?

Mr. Tisch: We have looked at the data and the data that we have been able to see has all been statistical data that has not convinced me that smoking causes death.

One certainly understands why Tisch and Horrigan want to believe the claims they are making. Their reasoning is understandable in light of the investments in place, but morally indefensible. In light of the enormous ethical difficulties facing the industry, the cleanest and least cumbersome strategy is to deny Premise B outright. The claim, however, that the evidence linking cigarette smoking to cancer is based merely on "statistical data" is simply outlandish. If Tisch and Horrigan were to testify before Congress that they do not know if the sun will rise tomorrow, it would be equally credible (or better, incredible). As the famous philosopher and economist David Hume pointed out, the evidence in support of this prediction is merely statistical as well.

A third component to the industry's strategy is to raise doubts about the conclusion of the syllogism. The industry might be willing to accept both premises A and B, but reject the implication that we have drawn.

According to the industry's argument, this conclusion is not a logical deduction from the premises, but an emotional (and, therefore, meaningless) appendage. Cigarette manufacturers do not cause harm; if harm is being caused, the smokers themselves are directly responsible.

This line of reasoning is by far the most important defense for the industry. Executives of tobacco corporations often emphasize that the choice of cigarette smoking is best left to the customer. The tobacco companies do not, and cannot, cause the harm. The consumer chooses to smoke, and, therefore, the consumer voluntarily chooses to accept the risks (if any) of smoking. This argument is similar to the argument put forth by the gun lobby; guns do not kill, people kill. Here, it is tobacco companies do not kill, smokers choose to commit suicide.

This argument shifts the responsibility away from the tobacco companies, asserting the producers are not directly responsible for the behavior of smokers. Therefore, tobacco firms, unlike heavy polluters, are not imposing harm on anyone, and are not violating tenets of CSR. Individual consumers should be given the sovereignty to choose whether or not they want to smoke. In exercising a market freedom, only the individual smoker can appropriately assess the benefits and risks of smoking.

It should be noted, however, that this counter-argument is rendered ineffectual by the tobacco industry itself. Individuals will make rational choices only in those situations where they have access to unbiased information. To the extent that executives of tobacco companies continue to insist that there is no proof linking cigarette smoking to health hazards, and to the degree that these companies continue to promote smoking among young people through sophisticated and misleading advertising campaigns, the tobacco industry will face ever increasing public scrutiny and presumably higher and higher legal costs.

On the face of it, it might seem that the actions and statements of executives in the tobacco industry undercut our observation above that in those cases where there exists a cause and effect link between corporate activities and the suffering of a particular group, it is almost universally accepted that corporations are expected to seek solutions. However, the extreme behavior of these executives, especially the testimony that no cause and effect link exists, actually supports our observation. Our point here is that even in the tobacco industry, executives accept the notion that if a cause and effect relationship were to exist, the industry would then have a responsibility to seek solutions. It is precisely because they accept this reasoning that executives are forced to paint themselves into a seemingly inescapable corner.

In some cases, the cause and effect relationship between corporate activities and harmful effects is well understood. This is certainly true in the tobacco industry discussed above. However, in many situations this is not the case.

As the relationship between corporate activities and harmful effects becomes more murky, the legitimacy of social responsibility programs becomes more fragile. Because of this, corporate decision makers need to evaluate carefully under what conditions proactive social responsibility programs can be defended. Justifying a proactive social responsibility program is an altogether different task than defending a corporation's decision to stop engaging in particular activities. In those situations where a corporation is not even indirectly responsible for causing a particular harm, managers must clearly articulate their reasons for expending corporate funds. Where little or no evidence exists to show a cause and effect relationship between corporate actions and harmful effects, the burden of proof shifts to corporate executives to be able to explain the benefits associated with a given proactive program. We, therefore, turn to a third criterion to evaluate CSR activities.

SHARED CONSENSUS AMONG STAKEHOLDERS

Often, an important condition for social responsibility programs is a relatively high degree of consensus among corporate stakeholders. This is especially true for proactive social responsibility programs that are designed to solve social problems for which the company cannot be held directly or indirectly responsible. If a corporation has not caused a particular harm, under what basis can it defend the use of shareholders' funds to finance a program designed to ameliorate the problem? The answer lies in developing a shared consensus among stakeholders, including shareholders. Cultivating a sense of common purpose among organizational players is a crucial strategy for effectively implementing such programs.

Educational reimbursement plans that provide an incentive for employees to continue their education or in-house training programs that enable employees to improve their job-related skills are not difficult to defend. These employee benefits can be justified along traditional strategic lines. Although these programs certainly promote socially responsible goals, the motivation for them need not be defended as such. Better educated employees will be more productive employees. However, scholarship programs for employees' children (or children in local communities) or "Adopt-a-School" programs are much more tenuous.

For years, General Electric has been involved with the Manhattan Center for Science and Mathematics. This program provides students from disadvantaged backgrounds an intensive college-preparatory high school program. Xerox has been offering grants-in-aid to veterans of the Peace Corps to encourage them to pursue teaching careers in the United States. Time Warner Inc. matches employee gifts to public schools. Pepsico has been a large contributor to dropout prevention programs (Council on Economic Priorities, 1991).

These individual programs are almost impossible to defend from a purely strategic viewpoint. Unquestionably, the interests of the economy as a whole are enhanced to the extent that these programs exist and are successful. However, it is difficult to believe that even the long-term financial success of General Electric, Xerox, Time Warner, or Pepsico would be harmed if any one of them discontinued their educational program. Whether Pepsico, for example, continues to sponsor dropout prevention programs will have no effect on Pepsico's financial performance, other than the direct costs of financing the project.

The problem we are alluding to is similar, but not identical, to the problem individual voters face. The probability of any one vote affecting the outcome of a major election is extremely remote. Nevertheless, society as a whole benefits from elections. Just as individuals recognize a responsibility to vote even though their vote will not make a difference, so, too, corporations recognize a responsibility to engage in proactive programs even though the company could just as easily not sponsor such programs.

There is, of course, a major distinction between the corporation and individual voters. Corporate executives are committing the corporation to engage in a form of altruistic behavior at no personal cost to themselves. In meeting perceived responsibilities, they are authorizing the use of the shareholders' funds. In some cases they may be influencing how employees spend their free time. Polaroid, for example, requires employees enrolled in their in-house literacy program to spend outside time learning to read. For this reason, it becomes more important for corporate executives to develop a shared consensus among all stakeholders. In order for the corporation to develop programs to combat social ills, decision makers need to assess the desires of all interested parties. Many programs like the educational initiatives discussed above are legitimated by a powerful consensus among corporate executives, shareholders, employees, customers, and local communities.

Managers need to communicate openly and effectively. Further, development of systems to register the interests of consumers and employees is integral to insuring that corporations develop decision-making procedures that reflect a general concern to behave well (Donaldson, 1982). Stakeholders must have input and should understand the purpose and goals of the CSR program. Further, all important constituents must view both the means and the ends of the program as acceptable activities for the corporation. At minimum, a successful CSR program will fit with the overall corporate strategy and culture. The better the fit, the more likely it will be that a shared consensus will emerge.

RELATIONSHIP TO FINANCIAL PERFORMANCE

Financial performance is a key variable in understanding social responsibility. As with all corporate decision making, managers must attempt to measure both the short- and long-run financial effects.

This is not to say that all CSR programs must satisfy the traditional cost-benefit criterion. Some CSR programs are justified in ethical terms, not in strategic terms. In situations where a high degree of knowledge and responsibility exists and where there is a direct and unambiguous link between corporate activities and social harm, the push for socially responsible solutions is mainly independent of financial considerations.

However, many, if not most, social responsibility programs are less clear-cut. Managers find themselves with less than perfect knowledge. Often, they are genuinely uncertain about the corporation's degree of responsibility and do not know to what extent constituents share their own perceptions. In these cases, the relationship between corporate social responsibility and financial performance becomes more important. Thus, managers attempt to justify social responsibility activities by explicitly linking them to a positive financial performance.

IBM, the giant computer manufacturer, provides a case in point. As IBM's proud profit history has receded into memory, its unprecedented financial losses (IBM generated more than $8 billion in losses in 1993) has forced the corporation to reexamine its once sacrosanct basic beliefs.

Underscoring the importance of the corporate vision, Thomas Watson, former chairman, once said that IBM is willing to change everything "except these basic beliefs." The most important of the beliefs was the company's insistence on the primacy of "respect for the individual." On the basis of both its words and actions, IBM became justifiably famous for its humane treatment of its employees (Pfeffer, 1994). Until recently, no one questioned the legitimacy of IBM's caring attitude toward its work force. In the current crisis environment, however, the hemorrhaging IBM and its new CEO have been forced to reevaluate human resource policies.

Critics are now raising difficult questions about the degree of responsibility a company like IBM has toward its employees. Further, the consensus supporting IBM's liberal policies has eroded. Responding to these changes in the external environment, the current chief executive,

Louis V. Gerstner, Jr., has revamped IBM's traditional beliefs. IBM's new altered principles read as follows:

1. The marketplace is the driving force behind everything we do.
2. At our core, we are a technology company with an overriding commitment to quality.
3. Our primary measures of success are customer satisfaction and shareholder value.
4. We operate as an entrepreneurial organization with a minimum of bureaucracy and a never-ending focus on productivity.
5. We never lose sight of our strategic vision.
6. We think and act with a sense of urgency.
7. Outstanding, dedicated people make it all happen, particularly when they work together as a team.
8. We are sensitive to the needs of all employees and to the communities in which we operate.

Importantly, the new principles continue to suggest a sensitivity "to the needs of all employees." However, the context of the statement and its location are telling. The emphasis has been altered. In the new environment, a "sense of urgency" permeates the corporation. The first principle unambiguously sets the tone; everything IBM does is driven by the marketplace. Thus, IBM's professed sensitivity to employees must be interpreted as a strategic decision to enhance corporate profits.

Is IBM's new set of principles hypocritical? On the one hand, IBM announces an unswerving commitment to shareholder value. On the other hand, the principles conclude with a salute to corporate social responsibility. IBM wants it both ways, shareholder value and a commitment to social responsibility. Some would have it that these goals are mutually exclusive. This view suggests that activities designed to increase shareholder value are outside the domain of social responsibility. If an activity is to be considered socially responsible, it must lead to a decrease in shareholder value. We believe this view is needlessly restrictive. Sensitivity to employee needs is both good business and represents socially responsible behavior.

IBM faces an environment that is beginning to ask important questions about the nature and contours of its responsibilities toward employees. IBM's traditional values are under increasing attack. A once powerful consensus has eroded. Our view is that IBM is not acting hypocritically when it couches its sensitivity to employees in strategic terms. IBM is attempting to balance the demands of shareholders against the needs of its employees. IBM's new principles reflect the CEO's belief that social responsibility, at least in the area of employee and community relations, causes better financial performance. By linking its human resource policies to shareholder value, IBM provides a strong and non-controversial motivation for social responsibility actions. IBM's experience demonstrates that under certain prescribed circumstances, CSR programs must be evaluated in view of the effects on financial performance.

We conclude this chapter by reviewing the four characteristics of the ideal social responsibility program.

Legitimate social responsibility programs are informed by a high degree of local knowledge.

They are designed to ameliorate problems for which the corporation is directly responsible.

All stakeholders are informed and agree about means and ends.

The socially responsible program will lead to enhanced financial performance.

No program will meet all of these standards. They are purposely couched as ideals to be pursued, rather than as minimalist goals to be obtained easily. Nevertheless, it is useful to examine some of the proposals for institutionalizing social responsibility against the backdrop of these criteria. In this way, we hope to learn more about each of the criteria and to understand more fully the relationship between the theory and practice of CSR.

7

Evaluating Specific Social Responsibility Projects

The previous chapter examined four criteria for evaluating the legitimacy of corporate social responsibility (CSR) activities. In this chapter we continue this discussion by applying these criteria to five specific institutional proposals designed to meet CSR goals: corporate charity, corporate codes of conduct, employee autonomy, worksite health promotion, and changing the structure of corporate boards. In this way, we shed further light on the criteria developed in the last chapter and are able to draw specific conclusions about some (but certainly not all) of the important institutional projects relevant to CSR.

CHARITABLE GIVING

An important mechanism for institutionalizing social responsibility is corporate charitable giving. The philanthropic activities of corporations are extremely significant to pro-social responsibility advocates for both practical and symbolic reasons. During 1992, U.S. corporations donated nearly $6 billion to charitable causes. Although this number represented a 1 percent decrease from the previous year, the first decline since the Depression, its sheer magnitude underscores the practical importance of charitable giving to our economy. Beyond the enormous material impact large contributions can have on local communities, corporate philanthropy serves a second function. By engaging in these activities, and through careful public relations, a corporation can successfully communicate its vision of corporate citizenship. Corporations donating a material percentage of pre-tax profits to charity (at least one company has a policy of donating 7.5 percent of income) weaken the traditional view that a corporation is merely a profit maximizing entity. A corporation engaged in significant charitable activity forcefully expresses a recognition of the existence of at least some social responsibilities.

Charitable giving has changed considerably over the past 100 years. Three stages in its evolution can be described. During the earliest stage, virtually no corporate philanthropy existed.[1] Corporate leaders began to recognize a responsibility as individual citizens to donate money to charity but were extremely hesitant to commit corporate funds for similar purposes.

Andrew Carnegie, recognizing the responsibilities of wealth while at the same time maintaining a sharp distinction between personal and corporate responsibilities, was one of the most important spokesmen for business leaders of the time. In his 1889 essay appropriately titled "The Gospel of Wealth," Carnegie noted that the man of wealth has a duty: "to consider all surplus revenues which comes to him simply as trust funds, which he is called upon to administer, and strictly bound as a matter of duty to administer in the manner which, in his judgment, is best calculated to produce the most beneficial results for the community — the man of wealth thus becoming the mere trustee and agent for his poorer brethren, bringing to their service his superior wisdom, experience, and ability to administer, doing for them better than they would or could do for themselves."

Julius Rosenwald's attitude toward philanthropy is seen as typical of the age (Fox, 1992). Rosenwald, who controlled more than 90 percent of Sears, Roebuck, and Co., became nationally known as a major philanthropist. He financed his activities from the wealth he amassed through his corporate dividends. Rosenwald, however, initiated only two charitable programs within the corporation. "The Agricultural Foundation, which grew out of his offer in 1912 to give $1,000 to any county that would raise the additional money required to employ a trained agricultural expert; and the Employee's Savings and Profit Sharing Pension Fund, which benefitted only Sears employees and their families. Rosenwald did not envision Sears, Roebuck, or other corporations, becoming leaders in charitable giving and philanthropy" (p. 105).

During the mid-twentieth century, the sharp distinction between personal and corporate responsibilities began to blur. U.S. corporations continued to grow. With the increase in size came an increase in economic, political, and cultural power as well. Increasingly, the inchoate notion of CSR began to take hold. Enormous corporations were wielding enormous powers. In this climate, corporate philanthropy came to be seen as a legitimate activity.

By 1950, the New Jersey legislature, formally recognizing the changing role of the corporation, passed the following law:

Corporations organized under the laws of this State should be specifically empowered to contribute such monies as, in a judgement of the governing boards, will conduce to the betterment of social and economic conditions, thereby permitting such corporations, as creations of this State, to discharge their obligations to society while, at the same time, reaping the benefits which essentially accrue to them through public recognition of their existence with the economic, social, as well as within the legal, structure of society.

Three years later, in the Smith Manufacturing case, the New Jersey Supreme Court was given the opportunity to determine the constitutionality of the new view. Judge J. C. Stein upheld the evolving view of the New Jersey legislature using bold and almost Biblical language.

I cannot conceive of any greater benefit to corporations in this country than to build, and continue to build, respect for, and adherence to, a system of free enterprise and a democratic government, the serious impairment of either of which may well spell the destruction of all corporate enterprises. Nothing that aids or promotes the growth and service of the American university or college in respect to matters herein discussed can possibly be anything short of direct benefit to every corporation in the land. The college-trained men and women are a ready reservoir from which industry may draw to satisfy its need for scientific or executive talent. It is no answer to say that a company is not so benefitted unless such need is immediate. A long-range view must be taken of the matter.

A small company today might be under no imperative requirement to engage the services of a research chemist or other scientist, but its growth in a few years may be such that it might have available an ample pool from which it may obtain the needed service. It must also be remembered that industry cannot function efficiently or enjoy development and expansion unless it has at all times the advantage of enlightened leadership and direction. The value of that kind of service depends in great measure upon the training, ideologies, and character of the personnel available. . . . What promotes the general good inescapably advances the corporate weal.

Finally, the decision concludes by noting that not only is corporate philanthropy a right of the corporation, but "it amounts to solemn duty" (quoted in Walton, 1992).

Clarence Walton, in his book *Corporate Encounters* (1992), described the change marked by the New Jersey law. According to Walton, the old Puritan tradition of personal responsibility, as articulated by Carnegie, of the rich toward the needy was being extended into an organizational responsibility to others who had no legal claims on it.

In this new environment, the chief executive officer played an exaggerated role. He might identify a pet cause, one that had little or no connection to the core activities of the business, and proceed to commit the corporation to donating relatively large sums of money. Craig Smith (1994) describes the second stage as follows: "When it came to selecting causes, corporate donors chose those least associated with their line of business. Bankers, for example, gave to the arts, and industrialists gave to sick children. But in the end, few companies concentrated their giving in one area" (p. 107).

Smith reserves his harshest criticism to the Exxon Corporation's "Education Foundation." Although it was widely admired for being independent, Smith notes that the programs funded by the foundation were unrelated to Exxon's main line of business. "Indeed, with outside directors and an ample endowment, the foundation conducted its giving program without considering the company's interests" (p. 108).

Richard Eells, a social responsibility advocate and consultant to General Electric writing in 1956, accurately described the second stage:

Philanthropy has a long and noble history, extending through many centuries and reaching into all countries. In the free American environment it has become stamped with a corporate character; and the rapid contemporary growth of corporation giving promises a new era in the long evolution of philanthropic work. . . . We have reached a stage in the evolution of corporate enterprise and the development of philanthropy where the two are meeting. The corporation has become a philanthropic force in the sheer bulk of its contributions.

In addition to this apt description, Eells also diagnosed with prescience the problems inherent in corporate philanthropy. He continued, the corporation "has yet, however, to establish itself as a leader in philanthropic endeavor. The reason for this lag is not merely the newness of the development. It lies rather in the failure to formulate a doctrinal basis for such leadership" (pp. 63–64).

Examining the legitimacy of corporate philanthropy, two important criticisms naturally emerge. Large gifts to charitable causes generally are not informed by a high degree of local knowledge. For example, banks that contribute funds to the local symphonies possess little or no special expertise about the arts. Second, charitable gifts generally are not designed to solve social problems for which the corporation shares any responsibility, even indirectly. If closing of a regional symphony orchestra is judged a social ill, it is inconceivable that a bank played any role in causing the symphony's demise. Thus, corporate philanthropy scores extremely low on two of the four characteristics discussed in the previous chapter.

These caveats against corporate philanthropy have been instrumental in altering our view of appropriate charitable activities. In response, a third stage in corporate giving has emerged. This stage has been labelled strategic philanthropy. Strategic philanthropy attempts to link charitable giving to financial performance. Judge Stein's assertion quoted above that "What promotes the general good inescapably advances the corporate weal" is certainly no longer taken as self-evident, if it ever was.

Outlining "The New Corporate Philanthropy," Craig Smith extols the virtues of strategic philanthropy. "Philanthropic and business units have joined forces to develop giving strategies that increase their name recognition among consumers, boost employee productivity, reduce R&D costs, overcome regulatory obstacles, and foster synergy among business units. In short, the strategic use of philanthropy has begun to give companies a powerful competitive edge" (p. 105).

According to Smith, philanthropy can do all this and still effect real social change. Corporations can play leadership roles in solving problems like school reform, hunger, community development, environmentalism, and AIDS awareness.

AT&T's charitable foundation, under the leadership of Reynold Levy, provides a model of the new paradigm. Levy insists that the foundation should not be viewed as "a thing apart." Rather, philanthropic activities can be designed to help promote business interests by forming alliances with the marketing, government affairs, research and development, and human resources function.

At AT&T, for example, it was Levy who suggested that the charitable foundation could help the marketing department project an image of the company as sponsors of the arts. Smith explains that it was the marketers' job to replace AT&T's traditional image with one more attractive to upscale consumers. "The foundation's arts specialists would use their expertise to select productions featuring the work of pathbreaking new artists who would appeal to the harshest critics and the most desirable potential customers" (p. 109). This successful, six-year-old program, called AT&T: OnStage, has allowed the company to rely less on advertising campaigns. Smith argues that this and similar innovative programs at the company give AT&T a competitive edge.

Strategic philanthropy is arguably more legitimate than earlier types of philanthropy. Perhaps this point can best be illustrated by examining AT&T's initiative on neighborhood day care centers for young children. At the urging of the philanthropic foundation, AT&T's human services division created a special fund that supports expanded day care in company neighborhoods.

This project has strong justification. First, AT&T, and, in particular, the human services division, is familiar with the day care problems faced by its predominately female work force. AT&T needs to attract motivated workers. To do so, the company needs to provide a convenient place to work. Enhancing the availability and quality of day care is an important step in this direction. Second, although no one would charge that AT&T is directly responsible for the difficulties faced by working parents, AT&T is well aware that those parents who choose to work for them are in need of some kind of day care solution. As argued in the previous chapter, this knowledge alone may constitute a certain level of responsibility. Third, a high degree of consensus exists among corporate stakeholders. The employee union at AT&T made it plain that family care should be included as part of the employee benefits package. Managers benefit by being able to attract from a wider pool of job applicants. Finally, shareholders benefit to the extent that better qualified employees can sustain and generate higher profit levels. The day care initiative, thus, scores high in terms of local knowledge, level of responsibility, shared consensus, and relationship to financial performance.

This discussion is not meant to imply that all strategic philanthropy is equally legitimate as a form of CSR. Reebok's "Human Rights Now!" concert tour with Sting and Bruce Springsteen, for example, might be justified from a financial perspective, but is surely irrelevant from a broader social view. Reebok possesses no special expertise in human rights. Further, the link between promoting a rock concert and solving international human rights abuses is hazy at best.

Nevertheless, the notion of strategic philanthropy remains an important development in the field of social responsibility. The process of executives searching for and implementing creative solutions to social problems touching upon the corporation helps promote a corporate culture embracing values beyond the bottom line.

CORPORATE CODES OF CONDUCT

During the late 1970s and early 1980s the majority of large U.S. corporations adopted codes of conduct (Brooks, 1989). Although the concept of corporate codes has a relatively long history (J. C. Penney has had one since 1913) its significance as a managerial tool is more recent. At the most general level, codes of conduct can potentially serve two major functions. First, codes identify and express concisely the mission or goals of the economic entity. Second, they represent a formal attempt by top executives to communicate expectations about acceptable employee behavior in meeting corporate goals. At minimum, the corporate code should help employees distinguish between ethical and unethical actions. An effective corporate code of conduct is both understandable and compelling.

In describing the specifics of corporate codes, it is difficult to draw a thumbnail sketch. Codes vary widely in length from 1 to 50 pages (Stevens, 1994). The content of codes differs from industry to industry. Size and firm specific circumstances can also influence the issues raised in a given code. Some evidence exists that firms in service-related fields are more likely to have a code.

The content of a code often reflects important circumstances existing at the time the code was originally composed. Because of this, a number of critics have pointed out that codes of conduct of U.S. corporations often focus on issues that have led to scandals. In a 1980 survey of 30 corporate codes, White and Montgomery (1980) reported that the most commonly addressed issue was conflict of interest (73 percent). Employees' responsibility to comply with federal law was second (67 percent), and misuse of corporate assets was third (67 percent). Sanderson and Varner (1984) report similar results. By contrast, Canadian firms are less likely than U.S. firms to focus on specific issues (Brooks, 1989).[2]

Landekich (1989), summarizing his research results, noted that specific regulations are discussed regularly in the codes. Among the legal issues frequently discussed, the author cites the Foreign Corrupt Practices Act, policies on affirmative action, equal employment opportunity, and antitrust and securities regulations. Perhaps the reason for the emphasis on regulatory and legal requirements is the fact that the courts often view these documents as binding. Because corporations can be held legally responsible for the actions of their employees, Stevens (1994) noted, "some ethical codes are little more than legal barriers and self-defense mechanisms" (p. 65).

Nevertheless, the best codes do not merely rehearse the legal responsibilities of employees, but often communicate a clear articulation of corporate goals. The code itself becomes an important rhetorical device providing employees with a sense of purpose. An effective code, like Johnson & Johnson's credo, quoted in part below, captures and symbolizes the core principles upon which the company was founded.

We believe our first responsibility is to the doctors, nurses and patients, to mothers and fathers and all others who use our products and services. In meeting their needs everything we do must be of high quality. We must constantly strive to reduce our costs in order to maintain reasonable prices. Customers' orders must be serviced promptly and accurately. Our suppliers and distributors must have an opportunity to make a fair profit.
  We are responsible to our employees. . . . We are responsible to the communities in which we live and work and to the world community as well. . . . Our final responsibility is to our stockholders. . . . When we operate according to these principles, the stockholders should realize a fair return. (Annual Report, 1993)

One of the most important benefits of a corporate code of conduct is the opportunity it provides for both executives and lower level employees to engage ethical problems before the fact. Brooks (1989) noted that many corporations are finding that discussion groups or case studies are helpful in fleshing out the meaning of their codes. The process of composing and interpreting codes can, thus, serve an important educational function. In this way, ethical problems and conflicts will be more easily recognized when they arise.
  A related benefit of codes is the fact that they signify an active rather than passive attitude toward corporate and employee ethics. Brooks argues that they represent an important move toward the management of corporate social performance rather than leaving it to happenstance.
  Landekich summarizes the benefit of corporate codes as follows:

Individuals have to be able to define themselves in terms of ethics, as they understand and feel it, if they are to attain a state of mind that leads spontaneously to ethical behavior. Similarly, as organizations of people working together, companies ought to be able to define themselves in terms of their ethics, if they are to attain a favorable ethical climate conducive to their overall success as business enterprises. . . . Company codes of ethics are suitable means of establishing and maintaining ethics-oriented organizational frameworks." (p. 89)

Thus, the existence of a well-publicized corporate code can help set a high moral tone for the company.[3]

Finally, an additional and less appreciated benefit associated with corporate codes derives from the fact that they are often available for public scrutiny. If so, codes can provide outsiders with an ability to evaluate professed standards of ethics.

An important question surrounding all corporate codes revolves around the issue of compliance. Simply put, why will employees accept the corporate definition of ethics? The codes themselves provide one answer. "Codes of ethics commonly include provisions for their administration and application. They also provide guidance regarding employee responsibility, violations, and disciplinary consequences" (Landekich, p. 57). Corporate ethics committees, compliance review boards, or the existence of "obudsmen" can also be helpful. Nevertheless, corporate guidance is usually sketchy. Detailed information about enforcement and implications of code violations is rare (White and Montgomery, 1980).

In light of the obvious difficulties involved in getting employees to comply with ethical codes, it is tempting to suggest that although they may reflect good intentions, corporate codes are meaningless, or worse yet, they are merely cynical attempts to manage the corporate image.

It is true that empirical evidence to rebut this suggestion is lacking (Stevens, 1994). Nevertheless, it may be unrealistic to expect positive empirical results at this stage in the research process. Questions about the effectiveness of corporate codes are extremely difficult to quantify. Therefore, Matthews's (1987) conclusion that it cannot be demonstrated that corporate codes cause enhanced social responsibility or create a corporate culture that promotes anti-criminal behavior patterns is not altogether surprising.

In defense of corporate codes, they are often informed by a high degree of local knowledge. For example, experienced managers can usually anticipate situations where conflicts of interest may arise. Further, corporations place employees in unique ethical situations. Although it is clear that employees willingly choose to accept these ethical challenges when they accept a particular job, corporations must recognize at least some level of responsibility. An acknowledgement of this responsibility leads to the creation of formal institutional mechanisms, like corporate codes of conduct, to help employees resolve ethical difficulties. Finally, and perhaps most importantly, the process of composing and interpreting codes of conduct — codes that communicate a meaningful vision of the corporation — instill a shared sense of purpose among corporate stakeholders. We conclude, therefore, that codes of conduct are important tools for shaping attitudes and behavior. A corporate code will be effective, not by warning employees about possible punishments, but by discovering and carefully articulating a set of core beliefs worthy of the employees.

EMPLOYEE AUTONOMY

There is a rising awareness of the importance of promoting increased employee autonomy within the corporation. Stamford University professor Jeffrey Pfeffer (1994) recently examined 16 managerial tools designed primarily to enlarge the role of the employee. Among some of his suggestions are the following:

enhance employment security,

pay higher wages,

reward performance with some form of contingent compensation,

increase employee ownership,

disclose more information to employees,

empower employees to enable them to participate in decision making,

encourage team work,

increase employee training and skill development,

make wage scales fairer, and

promote from within.

All of these suggestions recognize the inherent importance and rights of employees as human beings and, thus, fall within the rubric of CSR. Bruyn (1987), in discussing the idea of social investment, emphasized the centrality of employee autonomy.

Our position is that competition and cooperation are intricately involved in every organization, but cooperation provides the leading edge in development. Cooperation offers the basis for cultivating the self-governance and mutuality that fulfill human values in enterprise organization. Mutuality leads toward a sense of community within a firm, and self-governance leads toward individuality. Both attributes are prized by students of organizational development and can be evoked through cooperation. Competition remains important in the strain toward self-development, but there is still the question of whether effective forms of cooperation cannot achieve the same ends. The problem may be solved by learning the most effective methods of cooperation. (p. 48)

In evaluating the legitimacy of specific employee autonomy proposals, it is necessary to explicitly recognize the radical shift in perceptions that they entail. Accordingly, Pfeffer admits that his view "involves fundamentally altering how we think about the work force and the employment relationship. It means achieving success by working with people, not by replacing them or limiting the scope of their activities" (p. 16). Because of the radical nature of his suggestions, Pfeffer wisely chooses to defend them not as gifts to be bestowed upon the work force but as managerial tools to enhance the strategic position of the corporation. The title of Pfeffer's book is, therefore, well chosen: *Competitive Advantage Through People.*

It becomes necessary to defend these new managerial tools by linking them to long-term organizational performance precisely because of the lack of consensus surrounding these issues. The dominant American myth about human behavior, in general, and employee behavior, in particular, is encapsulated in the theories of Frederick Taylor:

1. The managers assume . . . the burden of gathering together all the traditional knowledge which in the past has been possessed by the workmen and then . . . reducing this knowledge to rules, laws, and formulae.
2. All possible brain work should be removed from the shop and centered in the planning . . . department.
3. The work of every workman is fully planned out by the management . . . and each man receives . . . complete . . . instructions, describing in detail the task which he is to accomplish, as well as the means to be used in doing the work. (quoted in Pfeffer, 1994, p. 126)

Taylorism asserts that employees can and should be managed much like capital equipment. It assumes that employees, given a choice, will always shirk rather than work, and that the employer/employee relationship is best characterized in adversarial terms. If employees win, the theory would have it, employers must necessarily lose. These views are codified in U.S. law, as well. Domestic training standards for employees are at the discretion of individual firms, while in most other industrialized countries they are encouraged by tax incentives. The use of temporary workers is not regulated in the United States, but is limited in amount and duration in other countries. Finally, health benefits are provided at the sole discretion of individual firms in the United States, but foreign governments, in many cases, either provide them or mandate the employers to provide them.

Because of these entrenched traditional beliefs about employee behaviors and attitudes, advocates for increased employee autonomy can in no way defend their views by assuming "a shared consensus." The argument for legitimacy needs to counter directly the assertion that employers and employees are locked in a zero-sum game.

After examining the automobile and textile industries, Pfeffer concludes: "The evidence from other industries and from the few cross-industry studies available confirms what we have seen in automobiles and textiles: there are invariably competing ways of managing the work force, and those that are consistent with producing a better employee relations environment, tend to be associated with improved performance on a number of dimensions" (p. 79).

Pfeffer's reading of the empirical record should not be surprising. The tasks organizations are called upon to execute are evolving. The knowledge worker is very different from the traditional factory worker. Peter Drucker (1993) artfully compares the new organizational structure to a symphony orchestra.

In the symphony orchestra, several hundred highly skilled musicians play together; but there is only one "executive," the conductor, with no intermediate layers between him (or her) and the orchestra members. This will be the organizational model for the new, information-based organizations. We will thus see a radical shift from the tradition in which performance was primarily rewarded by advancement into command position, that is, into managerial ranks. . . . We will increasingly see organizations operating like the jazz combo, in which leadership within the team shifts with specific assignment and is independent of the "rank" of each member. (p. 93)

The call for increased autonomy in the work force is a bedrock concept of CSR. It is arguably the single most important element in humanizing the corporation. Its legitimacy has been amply demonstrated by reasoned arguments and the existing empirical record.

WORKSITE HEALTH PROMOTION

The cost of health care in the United States continues to spiral out of control. "Increasingly all employers are experiencing uncontrolled medical costs which consistently exceed the overall Consumer Price Index and appear to be relatively immune to the economic containment strategies of utilization review" (Pelletier, 1991). As politicians and government officials continue debate about a national health care policy,

U.S. companies have begun to experiment with an innovative and important corporate strategy: worksite health promotion. The majority of large domestic corporations now have some type of health promotion activity in place. The most common are smoking control, health risk assessment, back care, and stress management (Breslow et al., 1990).

The basic assumption of health promotion is that employees, at all levels, often choose lifestyles that increase their probability of health related problems. If the corporation can help these employees alter their risky behaviors, employees would enjoy longer, healthier, and more productive lives. At the same time, by lowering the demand for health care services, the corporation might benefit from lower overall health related costs. Bly and colleagues, writing in the prestigious *Journal of the American Medical Association* (1986), suggest that corporate sponsorship of health promotion has been motivated by many factors, "including an interest in improving the health of employees, a desire to provide additional employee benefits, and a commitment to controlling health care, accident, and absenteeism costs" (p. 3235).

More than 10,000 epidemiological studies have documented a relationship between health risk factors and illnesses and injuries that account for over 75 percent of mortality in the United States. Further, the health literature shows that individuals with deleterious lifestyles experience higher health benefit costs than others. According to Goetzel and colleagues (1989), between 10 percent and 25 percent of total health care claims result from preventable lifestyle related costs. The authors suggested that heart disease alone causes 132 million lost work days and approximately $27 billion in lost work output. Fielding (1987) noted that one corporation estimated that each smoking employee averaged 25 percent more in health benefits costs than similar non-smoking employees.

Worksite health promotion is rarely discussed in the context of CSR, but as this discussion makes plain, under appropriate controls, it is a viable and legitimate institutional mechanism to alleviate an important social problem. The experiences of Union Pacific are revealing.

Union Pacific has had a long commitment to health promotion. Nevertheless, it has historically allocated only about 1 percent of its huge health care budget to prevention (in 1990, the company spent more than $360 million on health care). When it decided to adopt a more formal and more integrated health promotion program, the company needed both to determine which health risks should be targeted and what the overall impact on health costs would be. To quantify the projections, Union Pacific utilized the Lifestyle Claims Analysis (LCA) system from

Johnson & Johnson Health Management, Inc. According to a study by Leutzinger and colleagues (1993), the comprehensive methodology

> Involves analyzing health care claims and employee demographics and comparing the client's cost and usage with national norms and current research on disease risk factors. Using the client's actual demographics and claims experience means the result of the analysis can serve as a baseline for assessing cost and utilization trends over time.
>
> By examining treatments costs for 46 Lifestyle-Related Diagnosis Groups, researchers using the LCA can determine what proportion of medical costs exceeded the costs that would have been incurred in the absence of the 11 lifestyle factors involved.
>
> The LCA includes preventable costs, such as the portion of lung cancer costs attributable to smoking, but excludes non-lifestyle costs, such as the cost of lung cancer linked to environmental factors like radon (pp. 40–41).

In all, the statistical analysis examined the following 11 health characteristics and habits: tobacco use, alcohol abuse, elevated serum cholesterol, elevated blood pressure, motor vehicle and home safety, excess body fat, use of drugs other than alcohol and tobacco, inadequate exercise, stress, unsafe sexual behavior, and poor dietary habits. The results of the Union Pacific study indicated that the most costly lifestyle factor was stress. This one factor, according to the study, generated $35 million in excess medical costs. Overall, the study concluded that about 28 percent of the non-obstetric medical costs, or $87 million, were preventable. Leutzinger summarizes the implications: "The results of the LCA suggests that Union Pacific was likely to realize significant benefits by expanding its program of promoting health and preventing diseases and injuries. A comprehensive health promotion program called Project Health Track was implemented" (p. 42).

This project consists of three phases. First, all employees in four pilot areas were asked to participate in an initial screening to gauge various lifestyle characteristics. At this point, employees received immediate feedback on their need for improvement in a variety of areas. In addition, high risk employees were invited to participate in an intensive counseling program to address their specific health needs. A variety of classes and workshops covering specific health issues make up the third phase.

In evaluating the legitimacy of worksite health promotion, it is helpful to evaluate carefully each of the four criteria discussed in the previous chapter. As the example of Union Pacific illustrates, corporations have a strong built-in incentive to generate local knowledge about health problems and related costs. Other companies that have commissioned extensive research include AT&T Communications, Blue Cross Blue Shield of Indiana, Canada Life, Control Data Corporation, General Mills, Johnson & Johnson, Northern Telecom, Pacific Bell, Prudential Insurance, and Tenneco. Preventable costs for these companies, although not as extreme as the Union Pacific findings, have ranged between 9 percent and 19 percent. Health promotion, thus, meets the first criterion — local knowledge — discussed in the previous chapter.

Second, corporations, by asking employees to perform difficult and relatively dangerous tasks, must recognize a degree of responsibility for their employees. In fact, it has been suggested that health promotion initially grew out of an attempt to reduce the number and severity of work related injuries. Corporations began to train employees to avoid high risk situations (Breslow et al., 1990).

Health promotion as it is currently practiced, however, entails more than improving the safety of employees while on the job. Health promotion is designed to alter fundamental, and often the most private, behavior of employees. Therefore, the degree of corporate responsibility is a controversial aspect of health promotion.

In defense of health promotion, as argued earlier, the mere existence of knowledge about a particular harm may constitute a powerful argument for responsibility. In the case at hand, corporate knowledge about the dangers inherent in certain lifestyle choices and knowledge about ways to change employee behavior may provide sufficient grounds to justify health promotion. One might certainly question the ethical sensibilities of those managers who potentially could help employees at little cost to themselves or the corporation, but refused to do so on the grounds that the corporation was not directly responsible for employee behavior.

Unfortunately, the situation is a good deal more complicated. Critics of worksite health promotion point out many intrusive characteristics of the programs. It is often not clear by what criteria health care managers distinguish between employee behavior that affects the corporation (and is, therefore, a legitimate concern) and private behavior outside the domain of the employer. For example, can a corporation charge employees with children who choose to play soccer higher insurance premiums than other employees? Further, corporations have used data gathered through health care promotion against employees in workers' compensation cases. In order to receive insurance benefits, many employees sign release forms that give employers access to what many erroneously believe are confidential medical records.

As an example of how companies can misuse health promotion programs, the *Wall Street Journal* reported recently (May 18, 1994) how

Coors Ceramics, a subsidiary of the Adolph Coors Company, was able to exploit the medical history of one of its longtime employees, Richard Truman Fletcher, to defeat his wife's attempt to obtain survivor's benefits. Coors Ceramics obtained the detailed medical data through a health promotion program. According to the article, there is even evidence to suggest that employee assistance programs, a key element in health promotion, are being marketed as defensive tools to help reduce litigation. A monthly newsletter published by VMC Behavioral Healthcare Services, a purveyor of health promotion programs, advises its clients to refer employees to employee assistance programs and "leave a paper trail" (quoted in the *Wall Street Journal*).

This discussion, therefore, suggests two important qualifications about the legitimacy of health care promotion. Corporations need to ensure employees that the programs are purely voluntary and that medical information gathered through questionnaires and the like will remain confidential. Hershey's policy of mandatory medical testing and charging workers higher insurance premiums for certain medical and lifestyle characteristics is highly questionable from a social responsibility perspective. As Goetzel and colleagues have emphasized, successful health promotion is a function of respect for confidentiality.

In light of the above discussion, developing a shared consensus emerges as an important further justification. The desirability of health promotion requires an understanding and acceptance by numerous stakeholders. For example, Union Pacific management is correct in viewing its employee health care system as a "partnership with employees, labor organizations, third party health care providers, and its insurers."

Finally, much research has been devoted to testing the relationship between health promotion and financial performance in spite of the many difficulties associated with these tests. The argument for marketing such programs to corporate management will often hinge on the credibility of this evidence. The difficulties of measuring the effect of health care promotion center not only on measuring the benefits, which are both tangible and intangible, but also on measuring the costs. Often the cost of a health promotion program is not well documented and is buried in a number of different cost centers (Fielding, 1990). Warner (1990) further describes some of the difficulties associated with measuring the performance of health promotion programs:

One of the great handicaps confronting the would-be-health promotion program is that it is measured against a higher, more demanding standard than is conventional, treatment-oriented (and health insurance-covered) medical care. A medical care intervention simply has to represent accepted medical practice. By contrast, a health promotion intervention often has to prove its effectiveness (a standard not required of many surgical and medical prodecures), and its cost saving (never required of medical intervention). . . . Thus, as currently construed, the economic argument in health promotion implicitly forces the novel health promotion intervention to compete on the health side with established and insured patterns of medical care. On the fiscal side, it must vie with more effective restructuring of insurance benefits and delivery systems, each motivated exclusively by the desire to contain costs and neither needing to demonstrate a health outcome benefit. The proverbial deck is stacked against health promtion. (pp. 63–64)

Nevertheless, Pelletier and others who have studied the empirical record, even while noting limitations, have concluded that health care promotion does reduce medical costs. Documented evidence suggests health care promotion can reduce morbidity and mortality and can significantly improve employee absenteeism. In addition, health care promotion has been statistically linked to gains in employee productivity. Pelletier puts it succinctly, "In short, the answer to 'Do comprehensive worksite, health promoting programs save money?' is yes!" Interestingly, even with this optimistic conclusion, Pelletier hedges somewhat by observing that while the empirical record is impressive and sufficient for many decision makers, it cannot be the sole basis for adoption.

We conclude that worksite health care promotion is an intriguing and still developing idea. As with all decisions, each program needs to be carefully evaluated on its own terms. It is, therefore, difficult to draw broad generalizations. Nevertheless, in view of the four criteria for evaluating CSR, health promotion — assuming appropriate controls and respect of individual employee autonomy — is an important element in institutionalizing CSR. At its best, the corporation can play an important and vital role in educating employees about specific ways in which their health can be improved.

CHANGING THE CORPORATE BOARD

Corporate boards of directors can potentially play a pivotal role in promoting CSR. Boards of directors often possess the formal authority to effect real change in the corporation. For example, at its 1978 annual meeting, Control Data Corporation approved the following amendment to its corporate charter:

The Board of Directors of the Corporation, when evaluating any offer of another party to (a) make a tender or exchange offer for any equity security of the Corporation, (b) merge or consolidate the Corporation with another Corporation, or (c) purchase or otherwise acquire all or substantially all of the properties and assets of the Corporation, shall, in connection with the exercise of its judgment in determining what is in the best interests of the Corporation and its stockholders give due consideration to all relevant factors, including without limitation the social and economic effects on the employees, customers, suppliers and other constituents of the Corporation and its subsidiaries and on the communities in which the Corporation and its subsidiaries operate or are located. (Control Data Corporation, Proxy Statement, March 20, 1978)

Observers have pointed out that it is likely that, even in the absence of a formal amendment of this sort, management already possesses the power to assess social and economic effects (Schwartz, 1981). Nevertheless, corporate boards have come under intense scrutiny for being ineffective. Myles Mace, writing in the *Harvard Business Review* in 1972, strongly criticized the activities of corporate boards. "The lack of active discussions of major issues at typical Board meetings and the absence of discerning questions by Board members result in most Board meetings resembling the performance of traditional and well-established almost religious rituals. In most companies, it would be possible to write the minutes of a Board meeting in advance" (p. 42). Nearly two decades later, there was little reason to alter this view (Lorsch, 1989). While corporate boards are potentially important in the attempt to institutionalize social responsibility and possess the formal authority to effect change, in reality boards rarely have any impact.

Christopher Stone (1975) has put forth the most detailed potential solutions to this problem. Stone suggests a number of specific proposals to change the current structure of corporate boards. He suggests two sets of proposals: limited reforms and radical structural changes.

Among the limited reforms Stone suggests are the following:

1. Eliminate inside directors.
2. Choose at least some directors who have no financial interest in the corporation.
3. Clearly define the directors' functions.
4. Change standards for directors' liability to provide better incentives.
5. Provide directors with a staff.
6. Improve information systems to ensure that critical information gets to board members.

Implementing most or all of these suggestions, according to Stone, would improve CSR by reducing what he calls Class A behavior. This is behavior "regarding which there is a minimum of conflict between what the public at large would want, and what would likely be approved by a cross section of businessmen such as are sitting on the boards of typical major American corporations, if the board were fully informed of the fact." (p. 135). Included as part of Class A behavior would be inventory manipulations, racial discimination, manufacturing of unsafe products, corporate espionage, and gross environmental abuses. The key to the limited reforms is, as Stone makes plain, to make the board more representative of a cross section of businessmen and to modify the design of the board to improve incentives and increase information flows.

In contrast to these limited reforms, Stone also articulates a program for radical structural changes. He believes that every corporation in manufacturing, retailing, and transportation should have 10 percent of its directors "general public directors" (GPDs) for every billion dollars of assets or sales. GPDs would be nominated by a federal commission and approved by a majority of the board of the company. Using this rule, a significant number of companies would have GPDs exclusively.

In Stone's view, the most important function of GPDs would be to serve as the conscience of the corporation. Further, GPDs could assure that laws are being complied with, serve as liaisons in the legislative process, serve as checks on the effectiveness of fundamental internal systems, oversee the preparation of impacts studies, and act as information interfaces between the corporation and its environment.

Introducing GPDs would help reduce what Stone terms Class B behavior. Class B behavior, like Class A behavior, is behavior that allegedly violates the tenets of CSR. Stone defines it as follows. "Class B behavior involves cases where the public interest and the business community's interests are less overlapping: A cross section of businessmen such as are sitting on a typical major American corporation's board, even if fully informed of the facts, would quite likely not put an effective damper on the activities the public was against, nor put their weight behind those that the public favored" (p. 137). From this definition, it is clear why the limited reforms would be ineffective here.

Although Stone's limited reforms meet the criteria for evaluating the legitimacy of CSR and, therefore, should be encouraged, his proposal for radical structural changes fails our test. In other words, the notion of GPDs is itself problematic from a social responsibility perspective. The proposals are included as part of Stone's limited reform focus on increasing the production of local knowledge and are fundamentally predicated on a high degree of consensus among the stakeholders. By definition, there is a minimum of conflict about these issues. Further, the proposals are designed to reduce problems for which the corporation can be held directly responsible. As examples of Class A behavior, Stone included racial discrimination and the manufacuring of unsafe products. The limited reforms, therefore, easily meet the first three criteria developed above. By contrast, GPDs, designed to alleviate Class B behavior, are much more problematic.

Class B behavior exists only when the interests of stakeholders clash. By definition, Class B behavior is that behavior that the board, even when fully informed, feels is appropriate. The public would like to see such behavior eliminated. It is through the GPDs that the public interest is served. Therefore, the radical structural changes score very low in terms of both consensus among stakeholders and the degree of responsibility the corporation possesses (even while scoring relatively high in terms of the creation of local knowledge). Perhaps Stone himself recognized these problems. His ultimate defense of GPDs, oddly enough, is that their presence on the board will enhance the long-term financial performance of the firm. Stone is forced into this position. It is almost as if he must include this as his final argument to buttress his legitimacy claim. Even though the current board members and management would be opposed to the creation of GPDs, it really is in everyone's interests, even managers, shareholders, and current board members. Perhaps this is the case. But, as Stone leaves it, it is mere conjecture, and not very convincing. The legitimacy of Stone's more radical proposals are, therefore, called into question.

To conclude this section, Stone wisely chose to offer two sets of proposals: limited reforms and radical structural changes. Our examination indicates a strong case can be made for limited reforms, but his more radical structural changes rely on much more tenuous assumptions. His assertion about the link between GPDs and positive financial performance is necessary but needs additional justification if it is to be believed.

We summarize this chapter by briefly outlining our most important conclusions.

Charitable giving and employee autonomy are most powerfully legitimated by linking them to financial performance, especially where there is little consensus among stakeholders.

Corporate codes of conduct are often informed by a high degree of local knowledge. Further, the corporation has at least some level of responsibility for placing employees in unique ethical situations. Finally, they are useful in creating a shared sense of purpose among corporate stakeholders.

The degree of corporate responsibility with regard to health promotion is controversial. Nevertheless, in view of the four criteria for evaluating CSR — assuming appropriate controls and respect of individual autonomy — it is an important element in institutionalizing social responsibility.

Some of the less radical calls for reforming corporate boards are legitimate. However, the proposal to create general public directors directly contradicts the criterion of shared consensus. Stone's attempt to link this proposal to financial performance is not convincing.

NOTES

1.   Some exceptions exist. For example, railroads, recognizing the needs of their transient employees, became major benefactors and supporters of the Young Men's Christian Association movement. During World War I, corporations began donating funds to the War Drives and the Red Cross (Fox, 1992).

2.   See also Chatov (1980), Cressey and Moore (1984), and Matthews (1987).

3.   Not all corporate managers agree. Landekich reports the following responses by two corporate executives defending their choice not to develop a corporate code:

There has never been the slightest temptation to deal in a way that would or could tarnish the image of the company. . . . At the present time we do not have a published statement as to ethical business practices. In our particular case, we have found that this issue is best handled periodically at our regular management meetings. This gives top executives an opportunity to have a dialogue with the management level staff and, as a result, any potential misunderstanding would be clearly eliminated or dealt with at the time.

I doubt that dishonesty in the corporate area is any greater than in any other segment of our society. A number of people are crooks, larger number misconceive or don't understand the directions. . . . Enacting a rule without a will to enforce it, or if it can't be enforced because it costs too much to do so, possibly was fraudulently conceived. (p. 56)

8

Corporate Responsibilites beyond an Information Disclosure Policy

The last chapter evaluated the legitimacy of five specific social responsibility projects. In this chapter, we extend this discussion by examining corporate responsibilities in the area of information disclosure.

Accounting researchers are often reticent about offering normative guidelines to corporate managers. Most accounting research is self-described as a branch of "positive" economics. That is, the scientific agenda is to describe rather than to prescribe. Therefore, it is with great anticipation and interest that one approaches a recent article by Berkeley professor Baruch Lev where he adopts an unabashedly normative tone (1992). In this article he suggested that corporate executives involved in financial reporting activities need to evaluate their information disclosure decisions using cost-benefit analysis. He labelled his program "Information Disclosure Strategy." Throughout his analysis, Lev emphasized the need to view disclosure decisions as fundamentally similar to other corporate activities. Accordingly, he began his paper by noting: "Most importantly, disclosure activity does not differ in principle from other corporate activities, such as investment, production, and marketing. Disclosure shares with these activities the fundamental characteristics of providing benefits and incurring costs, and it therefore warrants the careful attention and long-term planning accorded to any major corporate activity. Hence the need for an information disclosure strategy" (p. 10). Similarly, he concluded his paper by summarizing, "Information disclosure is not inherently different from other corporate activities such as investment, production, and marketing, and it shares with such activities the fundamental characteristics of promising benefits and incurring costs" (p. 28). We strongly agree with Lev's conviction that disclosure activity "warrants the careful attention and long-term planning accorded to any major corporate activity." However, the purpose of this chapter is to suggest that weighing disclosure decisions only through the prism of cost-benefit analysis is not sufficient.

Most importantly, in formulating an information disclosure strategy, corporate executives must satisfy their obligation to report all information that is of sufficient importance to influence the judgment and decisions of an informed user. More specifically, the Financial Accounting Standards Board (1980) has warned that "the primary concern should be the relevance and reliability of the information that results." In addition, the Board explains, "Accounting information must report economic activity as faithfully as possible, without coloring the image it communicates for purpose of influencing behavior in *some particular direction*" (emphasis in original, p. 100). This well-known criterion is called neutrality. We consider it under the general rubric of corporate social responsibility (CSR) because it is binding as a guiding principle of action even if executives firmly believe that it is not in their best interests to release (or withhold) a particular piece of information, that is, even if the perceived costs to decision makers exceed perceived benefits.

The justifications for neutrality are threefold, corresponding to the first three criteria discussed in Chapter 6. Simply by virtue of the fact that they are making business decisions on a day-to-day basis, coupled with their access to all internal records, managers have an informational advantage over shareholders and other outsider groups. They, thus, possess local knowledge. Second, managers have a direct responsibility to shareholders to disclose in an open and neutral way. The withholding of information from shareholders is often tantamount to causing them direct financial harm. Finally, there is a high degree of consensus among all stakeholders, but especially among individual shareholders, concerning the importance of neutral financial disclosures (Epstein and Pava, 1993).

Our understanding of CSR corresponds with Archie Carroll's definition (1979). He writes that, in addition to economic and legal responsibilities, corporations must meet ethical requirements. "In recent years . . . ethical responsibilities have clearly been stressed — though debate continues as to what is and is not ethical. Suffice it to say that society has expectations of business over and above legal requirements" (p. 500). The fundamental assumption of this chapter is that corporate executives have an ethical obligation to report neutral information. This obligation can potentially conflict with economic goals.

Lev's analysis is reassuring and hopeful on two fronts. First, his example shows that accounting research can be linked in a meaningful way to practical issues facing corporate executives. Second, he convincingly shows that there is often great overlap between information strategies based on simple maximizing rules and neutrality.

However, we emphasize that the overlap is not exact. Simply put, a limitation of Lev's information disclosure strategy resides in the fact that it fails to recognize the possibility that what benefits most may not always coincide with what is right. CSR dictates that, regardless of the relationship between perceived costs and benefits, managers have an obligation to report information consistent with the principle of neutrality.

LEV'S ARGUMENT AND A CRITIQUE

The outline of Lev's basic argument can be summarized as follows:

1. Empirical research has shown that voluntary disclosures have material stock market effects.
2. Given that voluntary disclosures have effects, alert managers should formulate an information disclosure strategy.
3. The criterion that managers should adopt in formulating an information disclosure strategy is cost-benefit analysis.
4. Implementing cost-benefit analysis in the context of an information disclosure strategy leads to numerous gains.

Lev provides substantial evidence to support the first of the four observations listed above. Under the heading "The Impact of Voluntary Disclosure: Empirical Findings," he reviewed 13 empirical studies, which generally showed a positive stock market price reaction after the release of private information. Note, however, that not all the studies surveyed showed a positive price reaction. For example, Lev wrote that corporate warnings about impending litigation were associated with negative returns.

In summarizing this section of his paper, he conservatively drew four specific conclusions related to the empirical research studies.

1. Voluntary disclosures often have a significant impact on securities' prices and volumes of trade.

2. Information releases were found to be associated with enhanced liquidity of securities.

3. Despite seemingly strict regulation of financial disclosure, numerous choices are available to managers within the legal bounds.

4. Information disclosure, particularly of a prospective nature, is effective in changing perceptions even in large and active capital markets.

After listing these four conclusions, Lev extended his argument by suggesting that, because information disclosures do make a difference, alert managers should adopt an information disclosure strategy. This is the second of the four steps in Lev's argument. In his words, "Since investors' perceptions and the consequent market valuations are strongly affected by financial analysts following company securities, the 'management of analyst's expectations' should be of considerable importance to managers" (p. 13).

To this point there is no quarrel with his logic or reading of the literature. However, the link between the second and third steps of the argument is tenuous at best. Lev seems to imply that because there are similarities between information disclosure and other firm decisions, managers must adopt the same evaluation criterion, that is, cost-benefit analysis. Lev's clearest and least equivocal thoughts are found in the following two quotes: "The development of a disclosure strategy, as that of any other strategy, involves the evaluation of benefits . . . against costs. Costs of disclosure can be broadly classified into two categories: the direct costs of processing and disseminating the information; and the indirect costs, including those resulting from the impact of disclosures on company decisions and activities . . . the competitive position costs, and litigation costs" (p. 21). Although Lev recognizes the difficulty of implementing this strategy, he once again emphasizes its importance as follows:

In contrast to most other corporate activities for which objectives and costs can be straight forwardly determined, assessing these parameters for information disclosure is more intricate. This is largely due to the fact that information disclosure often exerts simultaneous and contradictory effects on various stakeholder groups. . . . Accordingly, the cost-benefit analysis of a disclosure strategy should simultaneously consider the effects of disclosures on all the firm's major stakeholders and constituents, including government and regulatory agencies. (p. 16)

It is left unargued how Lev moves from his reading of the empirical literature (which by design is purely descriptive) to his very specific, normative prescription suggesting that the criterion of cost-benefit analysis be used. The cost-benefit approach may conflict with the notion of neutrality. At minimum, Lev needs to more fully explain the logical reasoning that leads from the first two steps to the third.

Perhaps an examination of Lev's fourth observation softens the criticism. Lev explores a number of possible gains that flow from an implementation of his cost-benefit analysis. These ideas are sprinkled periodically throughout the paper. He states:

It should be appreciated at the outset that a disclosure strategy is not a separate, isolated strategy. Rather it should be integrated with the overall corporate strategy and culture. . . . Linked this way, an information disclosure strategy will be fully successful in assuring that securities' values and stakeholders' perceptions reflect the overall strategy of the company and the consequences of its activities. (p. 10)

Without an active, well planned and executed disclosure strategy there is no assurance that the intrinsic value of the company and its potential will be fully appreciated by outsiders (investors, suppliers, customers). (p. 12)

The major beneficiaries are, in general, the company' managers and its stakeholders. (p. 13)

A disclosure strategy that effectively disseminates timely, relevant, and credible information, allowing outsiders to evaluate the firm and its management in an effective low-cost manner, will not only narrow the information gap but will create shareholder value by decreasing the agency costs which depress values. (p. 15)

An even flow of credible information, as opposed to infrequent releases of highly surprising news, will decrease the volatility of security prices over time, further improving the risk and liquidity characteristics of securities. (p. 19)

Lev believes that, once managers view information in terms of cost-benefit analysis, they will be led to disseminate information in a "timely, relevant, and credible" way. Rather than volatile and suspect information releases, investors can expect "an even flow of credible information." He goes further by stating that, without an information disclosure strategy, "there is no assurance that the intrinsic value of the company . . . will be fully appreciated by outsiders." He implicitly promises that, with an information strategy in place, investors will be assured that the intrinsic value will be fully appreciated. As Lev notes, both the company's managers and stakeholders will benefit.

Once again the link between the promised benefits and his previous observations is weak. Why does Lev suppose that managers weighing the benefits and costs of their information disclosure policy will necessarily end up following a strategy that "effectively disseminates timely, relevant, and credible information?"

Lev himself recognizes that the existence of agency costs that serve to depress stock prices is a direct result of "managers' opportunistic, self-serving decisions" (p. 14). Advocating the position that managers must view information disclosure through cost-benefit analysis would only seem to worsen the agency problem, rather than relieve it as Lev contends.

To exacerbate the problem, Lev himself argues for the existence of a permanent information gap. If this is the case, why disclose in a forthright manner? "Economic theory has recognized that without active disclosure the 'truth' may never come out — a permanent information gap generally exists between insiders and outsiders" (p. 14). If one accepts the assumption of a permanent information gap, there is little incentive under the cost-benefit analysis for managers to publicly disclose bad news that they believe is not likely to be revealed through other sources. If there is a cost-benefit argument to disclose bad news that is viewed as part of the permanent information gap, Lev fails to make it.

To sharpen the critique, one might question two of Lev's specific suggestions concerning the formulation of what might be labelled biased accounting policy:

The financial reports of companies are the prime source of information for those looking for abnormally high profitability, market share gains, and other "suspect" corporate activities. This suggests the advisability of following a well-planned disclosure policy, such as the use of "conservative" (income depressing) accounting techniques. . . . Such an intervention-deterrent disclosure policy is particularly important for companies in politically-sensitive industries such as pharmaceutical, oil and gas, and utilities. (p. 20)

Lev seems to approve of the observation that, "Sometimes, accounting techniques are aimed at portraying a favorable managerial performance intended to affect takeovers or proxy contests" (p. 24).

Self-interested managers need to hide their abnormally high profits to avoid unwanted regulation. At other times, they have incentive to portray a "favorable managerial performance" to avoid hostile takeovers. It is not the point here to discuss the truth of these statements as descriptive of what actually occurs, but rather to question them as normative prescriptions. Are these suggestions consistent with the release of timely, high quality information? Viewing the information strategy as if it is merely the weighing of costs and benefits is not a sufficient criterion.

To be fair, at one point in the paper Lev himself seems to recognize the necessity of moving beyond cost-benefit analysis. "A temporary mis-valuation is, therefore, not an excuse for inaction, since managers have an implicit responsibility to investors to continually maintain market values as close as feasible to intrinsic ones" (p. 18). The recognition of this implicit responsibility, however, undercuts Lev's main thesis that decisions about information are fundamentally the same as other decisions involving investment, production, and marketing. Recognition of a responsibility to existing shareholders also seems to directly contradict his suggestion that executives should consider altering the shareholder mix to further management's interests. In general, given this implicit responsibility to report in such a way that continually maintains "market values as close as feasible to intrinsic ones," is there room for a cost-benefit analysis?

AN ALTERNATIVE APPROACH

One way of saving Lev's analysis is to view the disclosure problem as a familiar maximization problem, but subject to a full-disclosure con-straint. It is more useful to link the information strategy to the literature on CSR. Although Amitai Etzioni does not specifically use the term CSR, he provides a plausible alternative paradigm to the neo-classical assumption of utility maximization. His view, labelled socioeconomics, is consistent with a CSR perspective.

According to Etzioni, there is little evidence to suggest that investors and managers remove ethical and social constraints from executive decision making. There is even less data available to suggest that they should remove these constraints.

In his book, *The Moral Dimension: Toward A New Economics*, Amitai Etzioni (1988) presents convincing arguments and evidence for a more encompassing way of thinking about human motivations. He writes, "Those who study behavior in general, economic behavior in particular, should give up the assumption of a mono-utility world, propelled by one over-arching motive, pleasure, and recognize in their paradigm at least two irreducible sources of valuation or 'utility': pleasure and morality" (p. 21).

Intuition and the available evidence on fraudulent reporting suggest that managers should view information disclosure as part of a moral pull, rather than a self-interested push. First and foremost, managers need to view information strategy as a mechanism for meeting their obligation to provide complete and neutral information, as opposed to yet another opportunity to maximize firm profits.

THE CREDIBILITY GAP

Using financial disclosures as a tool to advance corporate interests can lead to questionable and outright fraudulent practices as the following recent cases suggest:

Now, considerable evidence suggests that IBM may have helped delay its day of reckoning with some surprisingly aggressive accounting moves. The moves didn't violate any laws or cause the company's fundamental business problems. Some, though not all, of the moves were fully disclosed to the public. But some finance experts say that just as IBM's business started to sour, its accounting became markedly less conservative. (*Wall Street Journal*, April 7, 1993)

A group of shareholders is suing Coopers & Lybrand and Giant Eagle, Inc., in addition to certain directors and current and former executives of Phar-Mor Inc., to recover losses on their investments in Phar-Mor and collect damages. The shareholders claim they were misled about Phar-Mor's financial condition when considering the company's stock. (*Wall Street Journal*, October 22, 1992)

How widespread is the damage? While survey studies conducted in the late 1970s, such as the Securities and Exchange Commission Advisory Committee's survey (1977) and the Neilson and Lind survey (1977), did not conclude there was a significant credibility problem, a number of more recent surveys have uncovered more disturbing results. For example, a Financial Executive Research Foundation study (1987) reported that 45 percent of individual investors agreed with the statement: "Annual reports would be more useful to me if they were less promotional." Eighty-six percent of investors agreed that "Annual reports are written to project the most favorable impression of company management." Even more disturbing, 85 percent agreed that "Annual reports would be more useful if the management was frank about reporting poor company performance." Finally, just 15 percent agreed that "Most annual reports are candid in their discussion of company performance." Each of these findings represents a strong indication of a credibility gap.

Hill and Knowlton, on the basis of their 1984, 1985, and 1986 surveys of professional and individual investors, similarly concluded that, despite the gains annual reporting has made in recent years, investors still do not believe what they read in many reports. The authors found:

Investors believe that annual reports often play down negative information and only report management's viewpoint. (79 percent)

Some investors outrightly distrust what they read in annual reports. (42 percent)

A number of investors complain that annual reports are too promotional. (58 percent)

Investors believe annual reports could be more useful by giving the bad news as well as the good news. (92 percent)

In addition, Louis Harris and Associates (1986) asked respondents to compare the level of honesty and integrity in business dealings today compared with ten years ago. Just over one in ten of the respondents said the situation was improving. By contrast, about 40 percent said the level of honesty and integrity was deteriorating.

Consistent with investors' increasing concern about the credibility of annual reports, Merchant (1987), in his study of fraudulent financial reporting, cited evidence that deceptive reporting may have become more widespread in recent years. Similarly, Pincus, Holder, and Mock recently concluded that, although the Security and Exchange Commission's current policies and activities related to fraud detection and enforcement are somewhat effective, participants in their study believed that there should be stiffer sanctions for registrant companies found to be involved in cases of fraudulent reporting. Finally, the *Report of the Commission on Fraudulent Financial Reporting* (National Commisison on Fraudulent Reporting, 1987), also known as the Treadway Commission, admitted that it is impossible to gauge the quantity of fraudulent reporting but, nevertheless, strongly urged management to improve the credibility of their reporting through adopting more stringent internal control procedures.

The findings reviewed above should be of major concern to those interested in preserving and enhancing the integrity and usefulness of financial reporting.

CONCLUSION

The ultimate goal of Lev's information disclosure strategy is praiseworthy. He states that, "Maintaining credibility requires a commitment to ongoing communication with outsiders, rather than haphazard disclosures under duress. . . . Credibility is predicated on a long-term, consistent disclosure strategy, where bad (i.e., below expectations) as well as good news are disclosed" (p. 26).

It is unlikely that a shift in focus on the part of corporate managers to a cost-benefit perspective will lead to such gains. Rather, it is imperative to emphasize the ethical component as well. The "management of analyst's expectations" can too easily be transformed into the manipulation of expectations. We, therefore, concur with Etzioni, who concluded his book with the following warning: "The more people accept the neoclassical paradigm as a guide for behavior, the more their ability to sustain a market economy is undermined" (p. 257). In many respects decisions about information dissemination are like other corporate decisions. Ultimately, however, they are unique. Although there is often a link between CSR and financial performance, as discussed in chapters 6 and 7, this chapter has amply demonstrated that this link is neither necessary nor sufficient for evaluating the legitimacy of CSR.

9

Conclusions: Ten Propositions about Corporate Social Responsibility

The purpose of this chapter is to succinctly articulate some general observations about the issue of corporate social responsibility (CSR). In selecting the ten propositions discussed here, our goal is to provide a summary of the most important implications of over 20 years of empirical and theoretical research. Although the discussion moves from less to more controversial aspects of CSR, we highlight those areas in which there is a high degree of consensus.

The task is both important and difficult precisely because there is so much that we do not know. It is almost impossible to define CSR, and even with a definition in hand, drawing precise policy and strategy implications is an overwhelming task (Wood, 1991). In 1971, the Committee for Economic Development provided an apt metaphor for CSR in comparing it to three concentric circles:

The inner circle includes the clear-cut basic responsibilities for the efficient execution of the economic function — products, jobs, and economic growth. The intermediate circle encompasses a responsibility to exercise this economic function with a sensitive awareness of changing social values and priorities: for example, with respect to environmental conservation, hiring, and relations with employees. . . . The outer circle outlines newly emerging and still amorphous responsibilities that business should assume to become more broadly involved in actively improving the social environment. (quoted in Carroll, 1979, p. 498)

More than 20 years later, it is still almost impossible to articulate a non-controversial set of prescriptive rules enabling us to know the relative sizes of each of the three concentric circles. The boundaries between the economic function and the legitimate social responsibilities of the corporation are still in dispute.

It is certainly true, as Wood recently noted in the introduction to her review of the topic, that our current definitions are "not entirely satisfactory" (p. 691). In spite of these difficulties, or perhaps because of them, it is the goal of this concluding chapter to emphasize and underscore the advances in our understanding of CSR.

For clarity and emphasis, we state our observations in the form of ten formal propositions. Our focus is on the relationship between CSR and traditional financial performance, but our coverage spills beyond this as well. Although there will continue to be constructive debates about CSR, the following general propositions are warranted.

At minimum, and regardless of ideological perspective, decision makers must begin to ask questions and understand the relationship between financial performance and corporate social responsibility.

Proponents and advocates of CSR consider this proposition as obviously true. Our point in emphasizing this proposition is that, even if one believes with the traditional view that in the corporate context ethical and social obligations are best achieved by the single-minded pursuit of profits, he or she should be aware that not everyone accepts this doctrine. A limitation of the traditional view is its seeming insistence on positing a fixed and unchanging legal and social environment. The reality is that, as new situations emerge and new and unique ethical problems arise, the rules of the game evolve. William Frederick (1976) captured this notion by describing it as "social responsiveness," as opposed to social responsibility. He wrote that, "Corporate social responsiveness refers to the capacity of a corporation to respond to social pressures. The literal act of responding, or of achieving a generally responsive posture, to society is the focus. . . . One searches the organization for mechanisms, procedures, arrangements, and behavioral patterns that, taken collectively, would mark the organization as more or less capable of responding to social pressures" (p. 6). Thus, for example, heavy polluters are increasingly required to bear more of the direct and indirect costs of environmental clean-up.

Therefore, the ability to predict social trends as well as financial trends, regardless of ideological perspective, is a necessary component to all managerial decisions. The traditional manager needs to avoid the ironic result that fixating solely on profits might result in less, not more profits.

Managers, board members, and investors are increasingly confronted by business decisions with social and, therefore, ethical implications.

As our economy begins to spill over domestic borders, corporations continue to expand in size, and technological effects multiply, society's well-being becomes more tightly linked with corporate decision making. As corporate power increases, the ramifications of its actions multiply. Many of the most important ethical decisions individuals face are within the corporate context. The executive decisions that ultimately led to the Exxon Valdez disaster were surely not only economic decisions (even if that is how they were framed by the principal actors) but also involved an ethical component as well. The question of whether or not a beer distillery should specifically target urban areas for a high-alcohol malt liquor must be answered with both economic and ethical criteria. The decision to continue marketing or to withdraw a record album advocating the killing of police officers, regardless of its solution, not only demands recourse to profit considerations but also requires a formulation and at least an implicit understanding of corporate obligations to society.

We emphasize this point, although it would seem obvious, because it is apparently not universally accepted. Milton Friedman (1962), for example, has explicitly stated that "The really important ethical problems are those that face an individual in a free society — what he should do with his freedom" (p. 12). We, of course, do not disagree that individuals face important ethical problems, but we believe that more and more ethical problems are faced by individuals within the corporate context.

A difference of opinion regarding social and ethical obligations does not prove that corporate social responsibility is unnecessary or perhaps (as some might suggest) meaningless.

Arguments against managers adopting CSR criteria often take the following form: Because it is obviously true that well-intentioned individuals disagree about CSR issue X, managers must, therefore, disregard issue X in formulating business policy Y. Once again, Friedman (1962) provides the clearest and most unequivocal formulation of this position. Friedman has written, "If businessmen do have social responsibility other than maximizing profits for stockholders, how are they to know what it is?" (p. 133). Friedman's succinct formulation captures one of the most difficult aspects related to CSR.

Advocates of this argument point out that managers are hired exclusively to maximize profits. Further, they have no special expertise in evaluating ethical considerations. Managers must, therefore, avoid arbitrarily usurping corporate funds in pursuit of subjective personal goals. An executive who pursues issue X is, therefore, in violation of his or her contract with employers.

We offer three observations. First, as has often been discussed by philosophers, an awareness and recognition of diversity of opinion and practice with regard to ethical issues does not imply ethical relativism. For example, the philosopher Robert Nozick (1981) has shown that, although it is not the intention of philosophy to produce uniformity of belief, nevertheless, good reasons can be put forth to show how there can be objective values and ethical truths.

If the traditionalist point is merely that it is difficult to precisely specify the contours of social responsibility, it is obviously true. If traditionalists are simply pointing out that we have not reached a consensus on many of the issues surrounding the ethical obligations of the business corporation, again, we would have no quarrel. If, however, the traditionalist view suggests that these reasons necessarily imply that social responsibility is an untenable option (as Friedman's position would seem to imply), it is unwarranted. The notion of CSR is difficult to implement in practice. This does not mean that it is impossible.

Second, even accepting the assumption that executives and investors explicitly agree that the sole legitimate corporate goal is profit maximization, it certainly does not follow that the ethical world, thus, evaporates. It is, at best, unclear why, if both parties to a transaction agree to disregard an ethical obligation, their joint obligation disappears. It may very well be the case that each of the parties may have an *a priori* and higher-level obligation to pursue issue X. Any contract, therefore, that supersedes X may not be binding from an ethical perspective.[1]

Finally, and perhaps most importantly, there is little evidence to suggest that investors and managers agree to remove ethical and social responsibility constraints from executive decision making. The assumption that corporate management cannot use ethical criteria in making good business decisions is at the core of the traditionalist view. It appears, on the face of it, that this is a strange suggestion.

Friedman has written that if social responsibility means anything at all it must mean that managers act in some way that is not in the interest of their employers. It is plausible, however, that investors are motivated to seek social responsibility goals. We suggest that, at minimum, the core assumption of the traditionalist argument — the single-minded pursuit of profits — should be subject to empirical investigation. Mulligan (1986) has summarized the counter-argument by stating, "There is no good reason why this remarkable claim must be true. The exercise of social responsibility in business suffers no diminishment in meaning or merit if the executive and his employers both understand their mutual interest to include a proactive social role and cooperate in undertaking that role" (p. 266). We articulate this alternative view as a separate proposition.

Some shareholders will willingly forfeit profits for enhanced corporate social responsibility performance.

Epstein and Pava (1992) have presented survey evidence consistent with this possibility. Though the stereotype is that investors are worried only about profits, when individual investors were explicitly asked to rank their preferences as to how corporate funds should be allocated, pollution control and product safety were rated significantly higher than increased dividends. Of course, survey results must be approached with caution. This is especially true when they are in direct conflict with frequent assertions like, "If investors have less than completely diversified portfolios, clearly owners would always prefer a company in which they had little or no interest to bear the cost for social investments with public or non-excludable benefits" (Keim, 1978, p. 35).

Nevertheless, our confidence is enhanced by comparing these survey results with similar findings. Etzioni reviews numerous studies that corroborate the idea that human beings can be seen to "act unselfishly." He reports that even neoclassical economists have been observed leaving tips at restaurants they do not expect to ever revisit. In experimental settings, subjects will return lost wallets at positive costs to themselves. Further, experimental subjects will not free ride; rather, they voluntarily pay "as much as 40 percent to 60 percent of what economists figured is due to the public till if the person was not to free ride at all" (p. 59). In prisoner's dilemma experiments, Etzioni concluded that "under most circumstances a significant proportion of the subjects do cooperate without being coerced or paid" (p. 60).

Intuition and the available evidence suggest that shareholders, even in their role as shareholders, behave much like the rest of us in terms of meeting perceived ethical as well as economic obligations.

Little empirical evidence exists that documents that firms rated high in terms of corporate social responsibility perform poorly in terms of financial performance.

In Part I we examined the long-term financial performance of a group of 53 firms that have been identified by the Council on Economic Priorities as being socially responsible and compared the financial performance of this group to a control sample matched by both size and industry (Council on Economic Priorities et al., 1991). We concluded by observing that there was almost no evidence that firms that are screened on the basis of social responsibility criteria performed worse than other firms. By contrast, there was some evidence to suggest a positive association between social responsibility and traditional financial performance. Further, there was little to suggest that the control sample performed relatively better in the later period compared to the social responsibility group. In fact, most of the evidence suggested that the socially responsible firms performed relatively stronger in the later period. This was particularly true for the market-based measures of performance but also held for one risk measure.

These findings are not unique. In Chapter 2, we identified 21 published empirical studies that attempted to gauge the degree of association between CSR and financial performance. Our single most important observation is that of the 21 studies, 12 reported a positive association between CSR and financial performance, 1 reported a negative association, and 8 reported no measurable association. As opposed to Ullmann (1985), we conclude that there is a consistent pattern in terms of this association. Although we agree with Ullmann when he wrote that "conflicting results were reported even in cases based on the same sample of firms" (p. 543), we strongly disagree with his interpretation that "no clear tendency can be found." While it is evidently true that not all studies report that CSR firms perform better than non-CSR firms, the overwhelming preponderance of the evidence indicates that CSR firms perform at least as well as other firms.

The doctrine of corporate social responsibility is not subversive to the economy.

"Few trends would so thoroughly undermine the very foundations of our free society as the acceptance by corporate officials of a social responsibility other than to make as much money for their stockholders as they possibly can. This is a fundamentally subversive doctrine" (Friedman, 1962, p. 133).

History has shown that Friedman's 30-year-old prediction, as captured in the above quotation, is false. To subvert, according to one definition in the *American Heritage Dictionary*, is to "destroy completely." Although it is difficult to reconstruct precisely what Friedman had in mind when he characterized CSR as such, a careful reading suggests two possibilities: CSR is subversive at the individual firm level or CSR is subversive at the level of the national economy. The fact that little empirical evidence exists to show that CSR firms perform badly would seem to undercut both of these interpretations.[2]

There is no necessary connection between corporate social responsibility and government intervention.

The motivation for CSR activities is in no way linked to increased government control over economic decisions. CSR is often carelessly classified with interventionist economic policies and programs. While many of the proponents of CSR also advocate government policies that limit corporate decision making and redistributionist solutions to perceived inequities, there is nothing inherent in CSR that would lead to these types of policies.

In fact, CSR would seem to be more closely related to a libertarian perspective. Most importantly, the concept of CSR must, at its foundation, emphasize the legitimate role of the corporation within the capitalist system. If corporate decision makers are to take the notion of social responsibility seriously, they need a serious understanding of the role of the corporation. They need a theory of the corporation that legitimizes it as a viable economic arrangement.

The ironic result is that CSR may lead to less government intervention, not more. In a society that more readily recognizes both the value and the limits associated with corporate behavior, one might expect a diminished call for government intervention in the marketplace.

Many forms of corporate social responsibility may enhance, not detract from, financial performance.

This proposition is the most controversial of our observations. However, we believe that it is the most consistent reading of the available empirical data. The conclusion is also intuitively appealing. This is especially true if by social responsibility we focus on the following core set of socially responsible activities: environmental pollution, employee and consumer relations, and product quality. Each of these areas is inextricably linked with financial performance.

What this last proposition does not imply is that corporations should go beyond their areas of expertise and solve social problems for which they are not even indirectly responsible.

The motivation for CSR can, thus, be an internal decision to increase long-term financial performance, while simultaneously meeting responsibilities for corporate effects. We conclude our discussion of this proposition by simply noting that it is supported by a growing literature.

Stakeholder theory, especially as developed by Ullmann, is a useful but not a complete paradigm to model corporate social responsibility.

Social responsibility does not cause enhanced financial performance; rather, financial performance allows for the performance of discretionary social actions. Much anecdotal evidence supports this view. Our conclusion, however, is that it may not be accurate to suggest that the demands for social responsibility are always external to the corporation, as the stakeholder model (as developed by Ullmann) implies.

To the extent that CSR enhances financial performance, it suggests a limitation of the stakeholder theory. As Ullmann (1985) has written, "Economic performance determines the relative weight of social demand and the attention it receives from top decision makers. In periods of low profitability and in situations of high debt, economic demands will have priority over social demands. . . . Economic performance influences the financial capability to undertake costly programs related to social demands." This model, however, which, *a priori*, ignores the possibility that the causal direction may also point in the opposite direction, is incompletely specified.

Corporations need to articulate corporate social responsibility goals clearly and unambiguously. Further, enhanced communication among all stakeholders would seem to be a necessary condition for implementing a corporate social responsibility program.

Nash (1990) convincingly argued that successful ethical decisions can more readily be reached if corporate goals, including social responsibility goals, are clearly articulated and widely known. Johnson &

Johnson's credo provides the most famous example. It states that the corporation has responsibilities toward its customers, employees, communities, and stockholders. Interestingly, the credo does not state an obligation to maximize profits but, rather, says that "business must make a sound profit." According to Nash, the existence and acceptance of this credo served to guide corporate executives during the 1982 Tylenol crisis in which several capsules were found to have been laced with cyanide.

Nash has described Johnson & Johnson's successful resolution of the Tylenol crisis as follows:

> Some outside managers have argued vehemently that there was nothing extraordinarily ethical or unusual about Johnson & Johnson's response. . . . I strongly disagree. Those who view the J&J response in these terms fail to account for and understand all the components of chairman James Burke's thought processes, not to mention those of the other managers who contributed to the two-hundred-plus decisions that had to be made in the first twenty-four hours of the crisis.
>
> Having personally interviewed the three top officers involved, I am certain that no textbook marketing analysis could quantify or even identify the factors that informed their strategy. From an economic and public relations standpoint one could have made the very reasonable argument for keeping the product on the shelves.
>
> ...
>
> As James Burke announced at the outset, Tylenol tested the very core of assumptions driving the firm's past success. Johnson & Johnson had always maintained explicitly in its Credo and implicitly in its advertising that its primary concern was for its customers. . . . Any strategy that hinted at a bias toward company profit over user interest or at the expense of public safety would deny these values. It would render the Credo claims dishonest and top management itself unreliable. In Burke's own words their first priority was to remain true to the Credo. (pp. 39–40)

What this case clearly shows is that the language of profits is useful but not sufficient in the corporate context. Executives, board members, and investors need to be able to talk about responsibilities as well. By clearly and unequivocally articulating its CSR goals, Johnson & Johnson arrived at what, in retrospect, was clearly the correct action.

CSR need not imply that executives act in some way that is not in the best interest of shareholders. To insure that executives can continue to satisfy shareholders, social responsibility goals need to be openly and effectively communicated to all stakeholders.

What makes this area of inquiry so interesting is that, with each answer, new and exciting questions emerge. The relationship between CSR and financial performance is complex and nuanced. This study has emphasized the recurrent and paradoxical finding that firms that have been perceived as having met social responsibility criteria have generally been shown to have financial performance at least on a par, if not better, than other firms. Although our understanding of CSR is by no means complete, it is our hope that this book has served to reinforce the belief that — despite the inherent complexity and intractability of the subject — this is an area of research that has proven to yield interesting and important results.

NOTES

1.   Nevertheless, the contract may be extremely relevant from a legal perspective. For a noncorporate example see Martin Luther King, "A Letter From a Birmingham Jail" (in Newton, 1989).

2.   A similarly dire description was put forth earlier by Theodore Levitt (1958) in the *Harvard Business Review*. The following brief quote underscores the exaggerated terms in which CSR activities were framed. "There is a name for this kind of encircling business ministry, and it pains me to use it. The name is fascism. It may not be the insidious, amoral, surrealistic fascism over which we fought World War II, or the corrupt and aggrandizing Latin American version, but the consequence will be a monolithic society in which the essentially narrow ethos of the business corporation is malignantly extended over everyone and everything." As we imagine even Levitt would agree, we are fortunate that his prediction proved false.

APPENDIXES

APPENDIX A
Summary of 21 Empirical Studies

Authors/Date	Social Responsibility Criteria	Financial Performance Criteria	Results	Comments
Bragdon and Martin, 1972	Council on Economic Priorities air and water pollution measures	Various measures of financial accounting returns	Lower levels of pollution were correlated with better financial performance. (+)	Authors correlated the pollution control indexes with profitability indexes (1965–1971) for 17 companies in the pulp and paper industry.
Vance, 1975	Milton Moskowitz's social responsibility ratings	Percentage change in stock price	All but one of the 14 firms in the sample had performance records considerably worse than the NYSE composite index. (−)	Author examined updated financial performance (1972–1975) of original Moskowitz sample.
Bowman and Haire, 1975	Proportion of annual report prose devoted to social responsibility issues	Return on equity	Mean return on equity for firms with "some discussion" was 14.3%, while the mean return on equity form firms with "no discussion" was 9.1%. (+)	Authors examined 82 firms in the food-processing industry between 1969 and 1973. Authors claim social disclosure is a surrogate for social responsibility. Some evidence provided which suggests relationship between social responsibility and financial performance may be U-shape.
Fogler and Nutt, 1975	Three pollution indexes	Financial accounting earnings and stock price data	No significant relationship was found between financial performance and pollution ratings. (0)	Authors examined performance of 9 firms between March 1971 and March 1972 after substantial publicity was released about their pollution tendencies.

Appendix A, continued

Authors/Date	Social Responsibility Criteria	Financial Performance Criteria	Results	Comments
Belkaoui, 1976	Disclosure of pollution control information in 1970 annual reports	Market-based returns adjusted for risk	The 50 experimental firms, in which pollution information was disclosed, out-performed the control sample in terms of stock returns. (+)	In the 4 month period following disclosure, the market made a temporary conversion of the positive effect of pollution control expenditures in higher share valuation.
Sturdivant and Ginter, 1977	Milton Moskowitz's social responsibility ratings	Ten year earnings per share growth	There was a significant difference in EPS growth between the best and worst social performers. Socially responsible firms outperformed their nonresponsible counterparts. (+)	Authors examined 28 firms between 1964 and 1974 who passed data requirements. They conclude that there is evidence that, in general, the responsively managed firms will enjoy better economic performance.
Alexander and Buchholz, 1978	Milton Moskowitz's social responsibility ratings	Market-based returns adjusted for risk	No significant relationship between social responsibility ratings and market-based returns. (0)	Authors examined stock market performance of 46 firms between 1970 and 1974. They concluded that their results are consistent with efficient markets. Further, the effects of the degree of social responsibility on stock prices were either non-existent or had occurred prior to 1970.
Chugh, Haneman, and Mahapatra, 1978	Firms belonging to high pollution industries	Market-based estimates of beta	Between 1970 and 1972 estimated betas of "polluter" firms shifted up. (+)	Authors compared 59 experimental firms, in high pollution industries, to 60 control firms. The authors attributed the shift in estimated betas to the increased water and air pollution control legislation during the 1970 to 1972 time period.

156

Study	Social disclosure measure	Performance measure	Findings	Description
Anderson and Frankle, 1980	Annual report disclosures (1972) related to social responsibility issues	Market-based returns adjusted for risk	In 6 month period following annual report disclosure there is no difference between disclosing and non-disclosing firms. Examination of March returns, however, gives credence to the possibility of a positive impact. (+)	Authors compared stock market returns between 210 disclosing firms and 113 non-disclosing firms. The authors concluded that the results strongly support the contention that the market values social disclosure positively. The ethical investor may exist and, in fact dominate the market.
Freedman and Jaggi, 1982	Council on Economic Priorities air and water pollution measures	Various measures of financial accounting returns	In general there is no association between pollution measures and financial performance. However, evidence is reported which suggests that for very large firms with poor economic performance, pollution disclosures are more detailed. (0)	The authors examined the relationship among pollution disclosures, pollution performance, and economic performance for 109 firms in highly polluting industries during 1973 and 1974.
Shane and Spicer, 1983	Council on Economic Priorities air and water pollution measures	Market-based returns adjusted for risk surrounding publication of CEP studies	The results indicated that the CEP firms experienced, on average, relatively large negative abnormal returns. Moreover, returns for those companies that revealed to have low pollution-control performance rankings were found, on average, to have significantly more negative returns than companies with high rankings. (+)	The authors examined stock market performance of 58 firms (pulp and paper, electric power, iron and steel, and petroleum industries only) between 1970 and 1975. The purpose of this paper was to investigate the question of potential information content of socially-oriented disclosures produced outside the firm.

Appendix A, continued

Authors/Date	Social Responsibility Criteria	Financial Performance Criteria	Results	Comments
Cochran and Wood, 1984	Milton Moskowitz's social responsibility ratings	Various measures of financial accounting based returns and excess market valuations	Firms with older assets have lower social responsibility ratings. There is also a marginally significant positive association between social responsibility and financial performance. (+)	Financial performance was examined for nearly 40 firms between 1970 and 1979.
Chen and Metcalf, 1984	Two pollution indices	Various measures of financial accounting based returns, estimated betas, and price earnings ratios	Controlling for firm size, there is no statistical association between pollution indices and financial indicators. (0)	In re-examining an earlier study by Spicer, the authors concluded that there is no relationship between a pollution index and financial indicators. The authors concluded that given the visibility of larger firms and the severe effects of pollution from large operations on the environment, a large firm tends to do more, either voluntarily or involuntarily, on pollution control.
Aupperle, Carroll, and Hatfield, 1985	CEOs' concern for society as reflected in mail questionnaire	Return on assets adjusted for risk	No significant relationships were found between a strong orientation toward social responsibility and financial performance. (0)	The authors examined the association between attitudes of CEOs (for 241 firms who were listed in Forbes 1981 Annual Directory and answered a mail questionnaire) and financial performance.

158

Study	Variable	Measure	Results	Description
Freedman and Jaggi, 1986	A pollution index	Market-based returns adjusted for risk surrounding annual report date	The test results did not indicate any difference between investor reaction to extensive disclosures and investor reaction to minimal disclosures. (0)	This study examines investors' differential reaction to extensive pollution disclosures in annual statements compared with those firms that make minimal disclosures. All 88 firms in belonging to chemical, paper and pulp, oil refining, and steel industries that disclosed some information were examined for 1973 and 1974.
Baldwin, Tower, Litvak, Karpen, Jackson, and McTigue, 1986	Investment in South Africa	Market-based estimates of beta	Excluding firms which do business with South Africa from investment portfolio produces a "minute" increase in risk.	Authors attempted to estimate the penalty (as non-market risk) that would have to be incurred as a result of not being able to invest in firms that do business with South Africa. The procedure was to delete excluded companies from S&P 500, and to then come up with the combination of stocks that eliminated the most non-market risk.
Rockness, Schlachter, and Rockness, 1986	Amount of chemical waste disposal as reported by EPA and US House Subcommittee on Oversight and Investigations	Various measures of financial accounting based returns	Higher ROE was associated with smaller amounts of on-site chemical waste disposal. (0)	This study examined 21 firms in the chemical industry between 1980–1983. It also examined the disclosure of environmental performance in the annual report with respect to hazardous waste disposal.
McGuire, Sundgren, and Schneeweis, 1988	Fortune magazine's annual survey of corporate reputations	Various measures of financial accounting based returns, market-based returns adjusted for risk, and market-based estimates of beta	ROA and total assets showed positive relationships and operating income growth had a negative correlation. Accounting and stock-market based risk measures tended to be negatively associated with social responsibility. (+)	The authors examined the association between financial performance and social responsibility for 98 firms during the 1977–1984 time period. The authors concluded that it may be more fruitful to consider financial performance as a variable influencing social responsibility than the reverse.

Appendix A, continued

Authors/Date	Social Responsibility Criteria	Financial Performance Criteria	Results	Comments
Cotrill, 1990	Fortune magazine's annual survey of corporate reputations	Market concentration, market share, industry	There was a positive association between market share and CSR. In addition, there was an industry effect as well. (+)	The author examined 118 firms in over 18 industries during 1982 and 1983. The author wrote that the biggest surprise was that the industry effect was not more fully accounted for by competition levels.
Patten, 1990	Sullivan Principles (A code of behavior mandating equal economic opportunities for non-white workers in South Africa)	Market-based returns adjusted for risk and trading volume around the signing of the principles	No price reaction. Authors did report a volume reaction. (0)	The author compared price and volume reaction between 37 firms who signed Sullivan principles in 1977 and 37 control firms. The results indicated that, at least in terms of volume, the information did impact upon stock market behavior.
Roberts, 1992	Council of Economic Priorities evaluations of social disclosure, dollars contributed by PACs, public affairs staff members, sponsorship of philanthropic foundation	Various measures of financial accounting based returns, market-based estimates of beta, size, etc.	There was a positive association between CSR and economic performance. (+)	The purpose of this study was to test "a stakeholder theory." The author examined 80 firms between 1984 and 1986 which met data requirements. The author concluded that the empirical results support stakeholder theory.

+ Denotes positive association between CSR and financial variables.
0 Denotes no association between CSR and financial variables.
– Denotes negative association between CSR and financial variables.

APPENDIX B.1
53 Socially Screened versus Control Firms

Rank	Socially Screened — Group 1	Control — Group 2
1	Apple Computer, Inc.	Tandy Corp.
2	Avon Products	Intl Flavors & Fragrances
3	Baxter International, Inc.	Smithkline Beecham PLC — ADS
4	Ben & Jerry's Homemade — CL A	Dreyer's Grand Ice Cream, Inc.
5	Brooklyn Union Gas Co.	Peoples Energy Corp.
6	Campbell Soup Co.	Unilever PLC — AMER SHRS
7	Chambers Development — CL A	Attwoods PLC — ADR
8	Clorox Co. — DEL	NCH Corp.
9	Cummins Engine	Brunswick Corp.
10	Dayton Hudson Corp.	Price Co.
11	Delta Airlines, Inc.	AMR Corp. — DEL
12	Digital Equipment	Hewlett-Packard Co.
13	Disney (Walt) Company	Bally Mfg. Corp.
14	Federal Express Corp.	Airborne Freight Corp.
15	Fuller (H. B.) Co.	Loctite Corp.
16	Gannett Co.	Times Mirror Co — DEL — SER A
17	General Mills, Inc.	Ralston Purina Co.
18	Hartmarx Corp.	Crystal Brands
19	Hawaiian Electric Inds.	Puget Sound Power & Light
20	Heinz (H. J.) Co.	CPC International, Inc.
21	Hershey Foods Corp.	Savannah Foods & Inds.
22	Houghton Mifflin Co.	Western Publishing Group, Inc.
23	Huffy Corp.	Harley-Davidson, Inc.
24	Johnson & Johnson	Bristol Myers Squibb
25	Eastman Kodak Co.	Canon, Inc. — ADR
26	Kellogg Co.	American Maize-Prods — CL A
27	K Mart Corp.	Coles Myer, Ltd. — ADR
28	Knight-Ridder, Inc.	New York Times Co. — CLA
29	Lifeline Systems, Inc.	Pico Products, Inc.
30	Liz Claiborne, Inc.	Benetton Group SPA — ADR NEW
31	Marion Merrell Dow, Inc.	Imcera Group, Inc.
32	Maytag Corp.	Whirlpool Corp.
33	Merck & Co.	American Home Products Corp.
34	Miller (Herman), Inc.	Kimball International — CL A
35	Nordstrom, Inc.	TJX Cos, Inc. — NEW

Appendix B.1, continued

Rank	Socially Screened — Group 1	Control — Group 2
36	Nynex Corp.	Bellsouth Corp.
37	Rubbermaid, Inc.	Illinois Tool Works
38	Penney (J. C.) Co.	Ito Yokado Co., Ltd. — ADR
39	Pitney Bowes, Inc.	General Binding Corp.
40	Polaroid Corp.	Ricoh Co., Ltd. — ADR
41	Procter & Gamble Co.	Colgate-Palmolive Co.
42	Quaker Oats Co.	Borden, Inc.
43	Rouse Co.	Vornado, Inc.
44	Ryder System, Inc.	Rollins Truck Leasing
45	Safety-Kleen Corp.	Sotheby's Holdings — CL A
46	Sara Lee Corp.	Smithfield Companies, Inc.
47	Stride Rite Corp.	Wolverine World Wide
48	Tennant Co.	Tokheim Corp.
49	Tootsie Roll Inds.	MEI Diversified, Inc.
50	Wal-Mart Stores	Woolworth Corp.
51	Wellman, Inc.	Courtaulds PLC — ADR
52	Weyerhaeuser Co.	Georgia-Pacific Corp.
53	Xerox Corp.	Fuji Photo Film — ADR

APPENDIX B.2
33 Socially Screened versus Control Firms

Rank	Socially Screened — Group 1	Control — Group 2
1	Baxter International Inc.	Smithkline Beecham PLC — ADS
2	Ben & Jerry's Homemade — CL A	Dreyer's Grand Ice Cream, Inc.
3	Clorox Co — DEL	NCH Corp.
4	Cummins Engine	Brunswick Corp.
5	Delta Air Lines, Inc.	AMR Corp — DEL
6	Federal Express Corp.	Airborne Freight Corp.
7	Fuller (H. B.) Co.	Loctite Corp.
8	Gannett Co.	Times Mirror Co. — DEL — SER A
9	Hawaiian Electric Inds.	Puget Sound Power & Light
10	Heinz (H. J.) Co.	CPC International, Inc.
11	Hershey Foods Corp.	Savannah Foods & Inds.
12	Houghton Mifflin Co.	Western Publishing Group, Inc.
13	Huffy Corp.	Harley-Davidson, Inc.
14	Kellogg Co.	American Maize-Prods — CL A
15	Knight-Ridder, Inc.	New York Times Co. — CLA
16	Eastman Kodak Co.	Canon, Inc. — ADR
17	Lifeline Systems, Inc.	Pico Products, Inc.
18	Maytag Corp.	Whirlpool Corp.
19	Merck & Co.	American Home Products Corp.
20	Miller (Herman), Inc.	Kimball International — CL A
21	Penney (J. C.) Co.	Ito Yokado Co., Ltd. — ADR
22	Pitney Bowes, Inc.	General Binding Corp.
23	Polaroid Corp.	Ricoh Co., Ltd. — ADR
24	Procter & Gamble Co.	Colgate-Palmolive Co.
25	Rouse Co.	Vornado, Inc.
26	Rubbermaid, Inc.	Illinois Tool Works
27	Ryder System, Inc.	Rollins Truck Leasing
28	Quaker Oats Co.	Borden, Inc.
29	Safety-Kleen Corp.	Sotheby's Holdings — CL A
30	Stride Rite Corp.	Wolverine World Wide
31	Tennant Co.	Tokheim Corp.
32	Tootsie Roll Inds.	MEI Diversified, Inc.
33	Weyerhaeuser Co.	Georgia-Pacific Corp.

Bibliography

Abbott, W. F., and Monsen, R. J. "On the Measurement of Corporate Social Responsiblity: Self-Reported Disclosures as a Method of Measuring Corporate Social Involvement." *Academy of Management Journal* 22(3) (1979): 501–15.

Alexander, G. J., and Buchholz, R. A. "Corporate Social Responsibility and Stock Market Performance." *Academy of Management Journal* 21 (September 1978): 479–86.

Altman, E. "Financial Ratios, Discriminant Analysis, and the Prediction of Corporate Bankruptcy." *Journal of Finance* (September 1968): 589–609.

American Accounting Association. *Report of the Committee on the Social Consequences of Accounting Information.* Sarasota, Fla.: American Accounting Association, 1978.

American Accounting Association. "Report of the Committee for Social Performance." *The Accounting Review* (Supplement to 50), (1975): 38–69.

American Accounting Association. "Report of the Committee on the Measurement of Social Costs." *The Accounting Review* (Supplement to 49), (1974): 99–113.

American Accounting Association. "Report of the Committee on Environmental Effects of Organizational Behavior." *The Accounting Review* (Supplement to 48), (1973): 73–119.

American Accounting Association. "Report of the Committee on Measurements of Effectiveness for Social Programs." *The Accounting Review* (Supplement to 47), (1972): 337–96.

American Accounting Association. "Report of the Committee on Non-financial Measures of Effectiveness." *The Accounting Review* (Supplement to 46), (1971).

American Heritage Dictionary, The: Second College Edition. Boston: Houghton Mifflin Company, 1985.

American Institute of Certified Public Accountants. *Report of the Committee on the Social Consequences of Accounting Information.* New York: AICPA, 1976.

American Institute of Certified Public Accountants. *Objectives of Financial Statements*. New York: AICPA, 1973.

American Jewish Congress. *Boycott Report: Developments and Trends Affecting the Arab Boycott and Arab Influence in the USA* 16(8) (October 1992).

Anderson, J. C., and Frankle, A. W. "Voluntary Social Reporting: An Iso-Beta Portfolio Analysis." *The Accounting Review* 55(3) (1980): 467–79.

Arlow, P., and Gannon, M. "Social Responsiveness, Corporate Structure, and Economic Performance." *Academy of Management Review* 7 (1982): 235–41.

Aupperle, K. E., Carroll, A. B., and Hatfield, J. D. "An Empirical Examination of the Relationship Between Corporate Social Responsibility and Profitability." *Academy of Management Journal* 28(2) (1985): 446–63.

Baldwin, S. A., Tower, J. W., Litvak, L., Karpen, J. F., with Jackson, H. F., and McTigue, B. *Pension Funds and Ethical Investment*. New York: Council on Economic Priorities, 1986.

Belkaoui, A. "The Impact of the Disclosure of the Environmental Effects of Organizational Behavior on the Market." *Financial Management* 5(4) (Winter 1976): 26–31.

Ben & Jerry's Annual Report, North Moretown, Vt., 1989.

Benston, G. J. "Accounting and Corporate Accountability." *Accounting, Organizations and Society* 7(2) (1982): 87–105.

Berger, P. *The Capitalist Revolution: Fifty Propositions About Prosperity, Equality, and Liberty*. New York: Basic Books, Inc., 1986.

Berle, A. A., and Means, G. C. *The Modern Corporation and Private Property*. New York: Macmillan, 1933.

Bly, J. L., Jones, R. C., and Richardson, J. E. "Impact of Worksite Health Promotion on Health Care Costs and Utilization." *Journal of the American Medical Association* 256 (1986): 3235–40.

Bowles, S., and Gintis, H. *Democracy & Capitalism: Property, Community and the Contraditions of Modern Social Thought*. New York: Basic Books, 1987.

Bowman, E. H. "Content Analysis of Annual Report for Corporate Strategy and Risk." *Interfaces* 14(1) (1984): 61–71.

Bowman, E. H., and Haire, M. A. "A Strategic Posture Toward Corporate Social Responsibility." *California Management Review* 18(2) (Winter 1975): 49–58.

Bragdon, J. H., and Marlin, J.A.T. "Is Pollution Profitable?" *Risk Management* 19(4) (1972): 9–18.

Breslow, L., Fielding, J., Herrman, A. A., and Wilbur, C. S. "Worksite Health Promotion: Its Evolution and the Johnson & Johnson Experience." *Preventive Medicine* 19 (1990): 13–21.

Brooks, L. J. "Corporate Codes of Ethics." *Journal of Business Ethics* 8 (1989): 117–29.

Bruyn, S. T. *The Field of Social Investment*. Cambridge: Cambridge University Press, 1987.

Buzby, S. L. and Falk, H. "A Survey of the Interest in Social Responsibility Information by Mutual Funds." *Accounting, Organizations and Society* 3/4 (1978): 23–27.

Carnegie, A. "The Gospel of Wealth." 1889. Reprinted in *The Responsibilities of Wealth*, edited by Dwight F. Burlingame. Bloomington: Indiana University Press, 1992.

Carroll, A. "A Three-Dimensional Conceptual Model of Corporate Performance." *Academy of Management Review* 4(4) (1979): 497–505.

Chatov, R. "What Corporate Ethics Statements Say." *California Management Review* 22(4) (1980): 20–29.

Chen, K. H. and Metcalf, R. W. "The Relationship Between Pollution Control Record and Financial Indicators Revisited." *The Accounting Review* 55(1) (1984): 168–177.

Chugh, L., Haneman, M., and Mahapatra, S. "Impact of Pollution Control Regulations on the Market Risk of Securities in the U.S." *Journal of Economic Studies* 5(1) (May 1978): 64–70.

Clark, J. M. "The Changing Basis of Economic Responsibility." *The Journal of Political Economy* 24(3) (1916): 209–29.

Cochran, P. L., and Wood, R. A. "Corporate Social Responsibility and Financial Performance." *Academy of Management Journal* 27(1) (1984): 42–56.

Coffey, B. S., and Fryxell, G. "Institutional Ownership of Stock and Dimensions of Corporate Social Performance: An Empirical Examination." *Journal of Business Ethics* 10 (1991): 437–44.

Control Data Corporation. *Proxy Statement*, North Arden Hills, Minn., March 20, 1978.

Cornell, B., and Shapiro, A. C. "Corporate Stakeholders and Corporate Finance." *Financial Management* 16 (1987): 5–14.

Cotrill, M. T. "Corporate Social Responsibility and the Marketplace." *Journal of Business Ethics* 9 (1990): 723–29.

Council on Economic Priorities and Alperson, M., Tepper Marlin, A., Schorsch, J., and Will, R. *The Better World Investment Guide*. Englewood Cliffs, N.J.: Prentice-Hall, 1991.

Cowen, S. S., Ferreri, L. B., and Parker, L. D. "The Impact of Corporate Characteristics on Social Responsibility Disclosure: A Typology and Frequency-Based Analysis." *Accounting, Organizations and Society* 12(2) (1987): 111–22.

Cressey, D., and Moore, C. A. "Managerial Values and Corporate Codes of Ethics." *California Management Review* 25 (1984): 53–77.

Dierkes, M., and Antal, A. B. "The Usefulness and Use of Social Reporting Information." *Accounting, Organizations and Society* 10(1) (1985): 29–34.

Donaldson, T. *Corporations and Morality*. Englewood Cliffs, N.J.: Prentice-Hall, 1982.

Drucker, P. F. *Post-Capitalist Society*. New York: Harper Busiess, 1993.

Drucker, P. F. "The New Society of Organizations." *Harvard Business Review* 70 (September–October 1992): 95–104.

Drucker, P. F. *The New Realities: In Government and Politics / In Economics and Business / In Society and World View*. New York: Harper & Row, 1989.

Eells, R. *Corporation Giving in a Free Society*. New York: Harper and Brothers, 1956.

Engel, D. L. "An Approach to Corporate Social Responsibility." *Stanford Law Review* 32(1) (1979): 1–97.

Epstein, M. J., and Pava, M. L. *The Shareholder's Use of Corporate Annual Reports*. Stamford, Conn.: JAI Press, 1993.

Epstein, M. J., and Pava, M. L. "Corporations and the Environment: Shareholders Demand Accountability." *USA Today Magazine* 121(2570) (November 1992): 32–33.

Etzioni, A. "Contemporary Liberals, Communitarians, and Individual Choices." In *Socio-Economics: Toward a New Synthesis*, edited by A. Etzioni and P. R.

Lawrence, pp. 59–73. Armonk, N.Y.: M. E. Sharpe, 1991.

Etzioni, A. *The Moral Dimension: Toward a New Economics.* New York: The Free Press, 1988.

Fielding, J. E. "Cost-Benefit and Cost-Effectiveness Analysis in Work-Place Health Promotion." In *Health at Work*, edited by S. M. Weiss, J. E. Fielding, and A. Baum. Hillsdale, N.J.: Erlbaum & Associates, 1990.

Fielding, J. E. "Economics and Worksite Health Promotion." In *Health and Fitness in the Workplace*, edited by Samuel H. Klarreich, pp. 270–83. New York: Praeger, 1987.

Financial Accounting Standards Board. *Statement of Financial Accounting Concepts No. 2. Qualitative Characteristics of Accounting Information.* Stamford, Conn.: Financial Accounting Standards Board, 1980.

Financial Accounting Standards Board. *Statement of Financial Accounting Concepts No. 1.* Stamford, Conn.: Financial Accounting Standards Board, 1978.

Financial Executives Research Foundation. *Investor Information Needs and the Annual Report.* Morristown, N.J.: Financial Executives Research Foundation, 1987.

Fogler, H. R., and Nutt, F. "A Note on Social Responsibility and Stock Valuation." *Academy of Management Journal* 18(1) (March 1975): 155–60.

Foster, G. *Financial Statement Analysis.* Englewood Cliffs, N.J.: Prentice-Hall, 1986.

Fox, K. "A Businessman's Philanthropic Creed: A Centennial Perspective on Carnegie's 'Gospel of Wealth'." In *The Responsibilities of Wealth*, edited by D. F. Burlingame. Bloomington: Indiana University Press, 1992.

Frederick, W. C. "From CSR1 to CSR2: The Maturing of Business-and-Society Thought." Working Paper No. 279, Graduate School of Business, University of Pittsburgh, 1976.

Freedman, M., and Jaggi, B. "An Analysis of the Impact of Corporate Pollution Disclosures Included in Annual Financial Statements on Investors' Decisions." *Advances in Public Interest Accounting* 1 (1986): 193–212.

Freedman, M., and Jaggi, B. "Pollution Disclosures, Pollution Performance and Economic Performance." *The International Journal of Management Science* 10(2) (1982): 167–76.

Friedman, B. M. (ed.) *New Challenges to the Role of Profit.* Lexington, Mass.: Lexington Books, 1978.

Friedman, M. "A Friedman Doctrine — The Social Responsibility of Business Is to Increase Its Profits." *The New York Times Magazine*, September 13, 1970, pp. 32–33 and 123–25.

Friedman, M. *Capitalism and Freedom.* Chicago: University of Chicago Press, 1962.

Friedman, M., and Friedman, R. *Free to Choose.* New York: Avon Books, 1980.

Gibbins, M., Richardson, A., and Waterhouse, J. "The Management of Corporate Financial Disclosure: Opportunism, Ritualism, Policies, and Processes." *Journal of Accounting Research* 28(1) (1990): 121–43.

Gilder, G. *The Spirit of Enterprise.* New York: Simon and Schuster, 1984.

Goetzel, R., Danaher, B., Fielding, J., Hillman, J., Knight, K., Wade, S., and Wilson, A. "Worksite Health Promotion: Review of the Literature and State of the Art Analysis." A Report prepared by Data Analysis & Evaluation Services, Johnson & Johnson Health Management, Inc., 1989.

Goodpaster, K. E. "Business Ethics and Stakeholder Analysis." *Quarterly Journal of Business Ethics* 1 (1991): 53–73.

Harris, L. & Associates. *A Survey of Perceptions, Knowledge, and Attitudes Towards CPAs and the Accounting Profession*. New York: Louis Harris & Associates, Inc., 1986.

Hawley, D. D. "Business Ethics and Social Responsibillity in Finance Instruction: An Abdication of Responsibility." *Journal of Business Ethics* 10 (1991): 711–21.

Heald, M. "Management's Responsibility to Society: The Growth of an Idea." *Business History Review* 31 (1957): 375–84.

Hill and Knowlton. *What Investors Want From Your Annual Report*. New York: Hill and Knowlton, 1988.

Ingram, R. W. "An Investigation of the Information Content of (Certain) Social Responsibility Disclosures." *Journal of Accounting Research* 16(2) (1978): 270–85.

Ingram, R. W., and Frazier, K. B. "Narrative Disclosures in Annual Reports." *Journal of Business Research* 11 (1983): 49–60.

Ingram, R. W., and Frazier, K. B. "Environmental Performance and Corporate Disclosure." *Journal of Accounting Research* 18(2) (1980): 614–22.

Jones, D. G. (ed.). *Business, Religion, and Ethics: Inquiry and Encounter*. Cambridge, Mass.: Oelgeschlager, Gunn & Hain, Inc., 1982.

Kahneman, D., Knetsch, J. L., and Thaler, R. H. "Fairness and Assumptions of Economics." *Journal of Business* 59(4) (1986): 285–300.

Keim, G. D. "Corporate Social Responsibility: An Assessment of the Enlightened Self-Interest Model." *Academy of Management Review* (1978): 32–39.

Kristol, I. *Two Cheers For Capitalism*. New York: Basic Books, 1978.

Landekich, S. *Corporate Codes of Conduct*. Montvale, N.J.: National Association of Accountants, 1989.

Leutzinger, J., Goetzel, R., Richling, D., and Wade, S. "Projecting the Impact of Health Promotion on Medical Costs." *Business & Health* (March 1993): 38–44.

Lev, B. "Information Disclosure Strategy." *California Management Review* 34 (Summer 1992): 9–30.

Levitt, T. "The Dangers of Social Responsibility." *Harvard Business Review* 36 (September–October 1958): 41–50.

Lindsay, A. D. *The Modern Democratic State*. New York: Oxford University Press, 1962.

Longstreth, B., and Rosenbloom, H. *Corporate Social Responsibility and the Institutional Investor*. New York: Praeger, 1973.

Lorsch, J. *Pawns or Potentates: The Reality of America's Corporate Boards*. Boston: Harvard Business School Press, 1989.

Mace, M. L. "The President and the Board of Directors." *Harvard Business Review* 50 (March-April 1972): 37–49.

MacIntyre, A. *After Virtue*. Notre Dame, Ind.: University of Notre Dame Press, 1981.

Marlin, A. T. "Shopping for a Better World." *Business and Society Review* 20(81) (1992): 32–33.

Mathews, M. R. *Socially Responsible Accounting*. London: Chapman & Hall, 1993.

Mathews, M. R. "Codes of Ethics: Organizational Behaviour and Misbehaviour." *Research in Corporate Social Performance* 9 (1987): 107–30.

McGuire, J., Sundgren, A. and Schneeweis, T. "Corporate Social Responsibility and Firm Financial Performance." *Academy of Management Journal* 31(4) (December 1988): 854–72.

Merchant, K. *Fraudulent and Questionable Financial Reporting: A Corporate Perspective*. Morristown, N.J.: Financial Executives Research Foundation, 1987.

Mulligan, T. "A Critique of Milton Friedman's Essay 'The Social Responsibility of Business Is to Increase Its Profits'." *Journal of Business Ethics* 5 (1986): 265–69.

Nash, L. *Good Intentions Aside: A Manager's Guide to Resolving Ethical Problems*. Boston, Mass.: Harvard Business School Press, 1990.

National Association of Accountants. "Report to the Committee on Accounting for Corporate Social Performance." *Management Accounting* 55 (February 1974): 39–41.

National Commission on Fraudulent Reporting. *Report of the Commission on Fraudulent Financial Reporting*. New York: AICPA, 1987.

Neilson, W., and Lind, G. *The Reluctant Marriage*. New York: Georgeson and Company and Lind Brothers, 1977.

Newton, L.. *Ethics in America: A Source Reader*. Englewood Cliffs, N.J.: Prentice-Hall, 1989.

Novak, M. *The Spirit of Democratic Capitalism*. New York: American Enterprise Institute and Simon and Schuster, 1982.

Nozick, R. *Philosophical Explanations*. Cambridge, Mass.: The Belknap Press of Harvard University Press, 1981.

Okun, A. *Equality and Efficiency: The Big Tradeoff*. Washington, D.C.: The Brookings Institution, 1975.

Patten, D. M. "The Market Reaction to Social Responsibility Disclosures: The Case of the Sullivan Principles Signings." *Accounting, Organizations and Society* 15(6) (1990): 575–87.

Pelletier, K. "A Review and Analysis of the Health and Cost Effective Outcome Studies of Comprehensive Health Promotion and Disease Prevention Programs." *American Journal of Health Promotion* (March–April 1991).

Pfeffer, J. *Competitive Advantage Through People: Unleashing the Power of the Work Force*. Boston: Harvard Business School Press, 1994.

Pincus, K., Holder, W., and Mock, T. *Reducing the Incidence of Fraudulent Financial Reporting: The Role of the Securities and Exchange Commission*. Report No. 3. Los Angeles: University of Southern California.

Preston, L. E. "Research on Corporate Social Reporting: Directions For Development." *Accounting, Organizations and Society* 6(3) (1981): 255–62.

Roberts, R. W. "Determinants of Corporate Social Responsibility Disclosure: An Application of Stakeholder Theory." *Accounting, Organizations and Society* 17(6) (1992): 595–612.

Rockness, J., Schlachter, P., and Rockness, H. "Hazardous Waste Disposal, Corporate Disclosure, and Financial Performance in the Chemical Industry." *Advances in Public Interest Accounting* 1 (1986): 167–91.

Rockness, J., and Williams, P. F. "A Descriptive Study of Social Responsibility Mutual Funds." *Accounting, Organizations and Society* 13(4) (1988): 397–411.

Sanderson, R., and Varner, I. I. "What's Wrong With Corporate Codes of Conduct?" *Management Accounting* 66 (1984): 28–35.

Schwartz, D. E. "Corporate Governance." In *Corporations and Their Critics*, edited by T. Bradshaw and D. Vogel. New York: McGraw-Hill, 1981.

Shane, P., and Spicer, B. "Market Response to Environmental Information Produced Outside the Firm." *The Accounting Review* 58(3) (July 1983): 521–38.

Smith, A. *An inquiry into the Nature and Causes of the Wealth of Nations.* New York: Modern Library, 1937.

Smith, C. "The New Corporate Philanthropy." *Harvard Business Review* 72 (May–June 1994): 105–16.

Social Investment Forum. *Socially Responsible Mutual Funds.* Minneapolis, Minn.: Social Investment Forum, 1991.

Spicer, B. H. "Investors, Corporate Social Performance and Information Disclosure: An Empirical Study." *Accounting Review* 55 (1978a): 94–111.

Spicer, B. H. "Market Risk, Accounting Data and Companies' Pollution Control Records." *Journal of Business, Finance and Accounting* 5 (1978b): 67–83.

Staw, B. M., McKenzie, P. I., and Puffer, S. M. "The Justification of Organizational Performance." *Administrative Science Quarterly* 28 (1983): 583–98.

Stevens, B. "An Analysis of Corporate Ethical Code Studies: Where Do We Go From Here?" *Journal of Business Ethics* 13 (1994): 63–69.

Stickney, C. P. *Financial Statement Analysis: A Strategic Perspective.* Orlando, Fla.: Harcourt Brace Jovanovich, 1990.

Stone, C. D. *Where the Law Ends.* New York: Harper & Row, 1975.

Sturdivant, F. D., and Ginter, J. L. "Corporate Social Responsiveness." *California Management Review* 19(3) (1977): 30–39.

Trotman, K., and Bradley, G. "Association Between Social Responsibility Disclosure and Characteristics of Companies." *Accounting, Organizations and Society* 6 (1981): 355–62.

Ullmann, A. A. "Data in Search of a Theory: A Critical Examination of the Relationships Among Social Performance, Social Disclosure, and Economic Performance of U.S. Firms." *Academy of Management Review* 10(3) (1985): 540–57.

Ullmann, A. A. "Corporate Social Reporting: Political Interests and Conflicts in Germany." *Accounting, Organizations and Society* 4(1/2) (1979): 123–33.

U.S. Securities and Exchange Commission, Advisory Committee on Corporate Disclosure. *Report of the Advisory Committee on Corporate Disclosure to the Securities and Exchange Commission. Volumes 1 and 2, November 3, 1977.* Washington, D.C.: U.S. Government Printing Office, 1977.

Vance, S. C. "Are Socially Responsible Corporations Good Investment Risks?" *Management Review* 64(8) (1975): 18–24.

Walton, C. *The Moral Manager.* New York: Harper & Row, 1988.

Walton, C. *Corporate Encounters: Ethics, Law, and Business Environment.* Forth Worth, Tex.: The Dryden Press, 1992.

Warner, K. E. "Wellness at the Worksite." *Health Affairs: Promoting Health* (Summer 1990): 63–79.

White, B., and Montgomery, R. "Corporate Codes of Conduct." *California Management Review* 23(2) (1980): 80–87.

Wiseman, J. "An Evaluation of Environmental Disclosures Made in Corporate Annual Reports." *Accounting, Organizations and Society* 7(1) (1982): 53–63.

Wolfe, R. "The Use of Content Analysis To Assess Corporate Social Responsibility." *Research in Corporate Social Performance and Policy* 12 (1991): 281–307.

Wood, D. J. *Business and Society*. New York: Harper Collins, 1994.
Wood, D. J. "Corporate Social Performance Revisited." *Academy of Management
    Review* 16(4) (1991): 691–718.

Index

ABOUT THE AUTHORS

MOSES L. PAVA is currently Associate Professor of Accounting and holds the Alvin H. Einbender Chair in Business Ethics at the Sy Syms School of Business, Yeshiva University. He is the author of numerous articles on financial disclosures and corporate social responsibility and is author of *The Shareholder's Use of Corporate Annual Reports* (1993).

JOSHUA KRAUSZ is Gershon and Merle Stern Professor of Banking and Finance at the Sy Syms School of Business, Yeshiva University. His research interests include financial analysis, ethics and social responsibility, financial accounting, options and derivatives, price behavior, capital budgeting, and taxation.